"A Lot of Firsts"

By

Paul Schissler

Published May 2019

www.paulschissler.com

Dedicated to my superhero wife. You're my home and my person. And to my son, I'm so grateful that I get to be your dad.

My First Shirtless Audition

I went on an audition for a commercial. I had to take my shirt off. Oh no. (I kept my wedding ring on). But I'm self-conscious about my big nipples. I haven't worn a white t-shirt since I was in kindergarten. If I want to wear a white t-shirt I have to layer another one to two shirts underneath so that you don't see my nips staring you in the face. I didn't know I had big nipples until my brother pointed them out.

"You got some pepperonis."

"What?"

"Your nipples. They're huge. They're like National Geographic-sized nipples. Like you're an indigenous--"

"I got it."

"Big ol--"

"I GOT IT. You're an idiot, we have the same size nipples."

"Nah, yours are bigger."

Just two brothers, bonding.

From then on, anytime I took my shirt off at the pool or the beach, I was paranoid everyone was whispering about the dinner plates on my chest. I'm not like one of those lucky bastards with little dime-sized nips.

It's like when God was making me in Heaven, He was also in the middle of making a pepperoni pizza and he got a little distracted. Threw down a couple pepperonis on my chest, two nipples on a pizza and next thing you know, BAM. Some angel's chowing down on a nightmare of a pizza while a middle school boy is covering his nipples at the pool like some prude.

I told my wife I was nervous about taking off my shirt in front of the casting director. They're going to see my huge nipples and vomit. She consoled me. My loving, supportive wife, who only sees the best in me and constantly affirms me. Builds me up and makes me feel confident about who I am. She said, "oh stop, you don't have big nipples, you have big areolas."

OH WHEW.

Turns out I have big areolas AND I'm dumb. My whole life I couldn't even distinguish between the nipple and the areola. But what a relief that I have the bigger of the two that takes up the most real estate on my chest.

They had me stand in the room while the guy before me auditioned. He took off his shirt. I almost started to applaud. It looked like he photoshopped Zac Efron's body onto his body. Perfectly shaped nipples. Manly-sized areolas. That jerk. Good for him. I should've left right there.

Now it was my turn. I took off my shirt. My areolas flaunting in all their glory. It was cold so for a brief second my areolas shrank slightly smaller. The casting director got an eye full of pale skin, moles and pepperoni. You're welcome. Soak it in, sir. Almost as soon as I tossed my shirt aside the director said, "THANKS SO MUCH."

I gathered my shirt and threw it on like an ashamed hooker. Look. At the end of the day, I'm happy with my body. The lesson here is never, NEVER look at the guy auditioning before you.

The First Time Waking Up My Wife with a Fart

Okay. I woke up my wife with a fart. I know. I KNOW. Not proud. (It may have happened more than once.)

She's a deep sleeper. I could set off fireworks in the bedroom and blast death metal music and she would still sleep. Here's the thing. It was not the *sound* of the fart that woke her up. (I KNOW.)

The *smell* literally broke her out of a REM cycle. You know in the movies when you see someone come back to life after they were drowning? It was like that. But instead of coming back to life, she woke up to death. It did NOT smell fresh.

I know it was bad, because this is what she said when she woke up:

"OH MY--- baby, why do you hate me?"
Thankfully, I'm quick on my feet.

"You smell that too?"

Death stare.

"Why would you do that? It's so noxious. You ruined our bed."

"Ok, I mean it's not tha--"

"It's the worst thing I've ever smelled in my life. Why would you do that to your wife?"

Spousal violence apparently comes in many forms. Never thought I'd fart so bad I'd need marriage counseling. WOW. Now anytime I have gas I have to leave the bedroom. THE THINGS WE DO FOR LOVE. Doctors say it's healthy to release gas when you have it, but what they don't tell you is that it's bad for relationships.

Babymoon Gone Wrong Then Right

Wife and I were planning to go to Greece (the real Greece, not Astoria). The first two announcements about delays gave me heartburn. They gave everyone free food to console our furious animal brains. After waiting 10 hours they announce there's a maintenance issue and the flight is cancelled. Everyone blacks out with rage. At this point I don't even remember what the word 'patience' means. I'm a big ole pouting baby. Wife is frantically getting refunds on all Greece bookings. To helpfully contribute to our situation I continue to stress eat. They announce the next three days of Greece flights are overbooked (classic). At this point passengers have formed their alliances, broken off handles from rolling suitcases as weapons and are on the verge of full out riot. It's 'Lord of the Flies' but with overweight adults and tacky Hawaiian shirts. Also, we were flying out of Philly so we couldn't just go home (double classic). A dear friend from Philly let us crash for the night. Get good friends in your life like that if you don't have them.

We found that there were open seats on a flight to Venice. VERY awesome plan B destination. Wife frantically booked hotels. While she whipped together an entirely new itinerary, I helped out by eating junk food. Got on a plane to Italy and now we're here butchering the lovely language by saying things like "more gelato, grat-see". Pretty sure I've said "chef boyardee" twice on accident (once on purpose).

Through all this we learned sometimes in life you do weeks of planning to go to a certain place but it doesn't work out, things fall through, but you end up somewhere beautiful. No plans, just present in the moment.

Earning My Brother-in-law's Respect

It was a pleasant evening. My wife and I had her older brother and his daughter over for dinner. It was nice. I love my brother-in-law. He's one of the best guys I know and we get along lovely. BUT he's also the most alpha male I've ever met in my life. Not only does he have a successful career in finance, but he does IRONMAN COMPETITIONS. I can't even run two miles before giving up and calling a cab.

We finish dinner and my bro-in-law commented that I'm looking pretty strong. Do I work out? How much do I bench? (Classic bro talk).

Then my well-meaning, fiercely supportive, encouraging wife says, "I bet Paul's stronger than you."

To which I replied, "<SILENCE FOR 10 SECONDS>"

To which my bro-in-law responded, "Oh yeah? Let's arm wrestle."

THANK YOU SO MUCH HONEY. I'm in panic mode. I don't want to arm wrestle. I hate conflict. I can't lose an arm wrestle IN MY OWN HOME. Internally, I'm hyping myself up like I'm going into battle: "you must defend your home, you must defend your wife's honor, you must earn your bro's respect by beating him in front of his daughter and sister. DO. NOT. LOSE." All really healthy, post-dinner thoughts.

I agree to the arm wrestle. We get on our knees and post up on the coffee table. Wife and bro-in-law are laughing and chatting. I am silent. I am in the zone. Channeling all of my fear strength.

BEGIN. We are locked in and in a stalemate for a good five seconds. Wavering side to side. The whole time in my head I'm screaming at myself "DEFEND YOUR WIFE'S HONOR. DEFEND YOUR HOME." I've never had an adrenaline rush before, but about ten seconds into the match, I have a burst like a mother lifting a car off her baby. I slam him down. Thank you merciful God for giving me the strength to win and continue making eye contact with my brother-in-law for the rest of our lives.

As soon as I won the match he left. Awkwardest goodbye ever. I've retired from arm wrestling forever.

My First Night in NYC

Yikes.

I was crashing with one of my sister-in-law's friends in Brooklyn. It was January and rainy. I had been in Manhattan hanging out with a friend from college and when I returned to Brooklyn it was a little before midnight, cold and rainy. I buzzed the door. Nothing.
I buzzed again. Nothing.

I text. Nothing.

I call. Nothing.

Waited 15 minutes. Then repeated the cycle.

Buzz.

Text.

Call.

Nothing.

OH GOOD.

I keep doing this for a few hours. Luckily, I'm sitting on the front steps in cold rain. So blessed.

PANIC SETS IN. At this point it's now 2:00AM. A few drunk people who live in the building come home and let me inside. Thank God. I'm out of the cold rain. Finally I can go to bed and get some rest for my first day of work as a busboy at a fancy Italian restaurant (I quit this job after three days because it was too stressful).

I knock. Nothing.
I ring. Nothing.
I text and call. Nothing.
[Repeat for two hours].
NOTHING. OH DEAR GOD.

I feel like a psycho ex-boyfriend. I don't know what else to do. So I do the only rational thing I know to do. I sit down in the stairwell and wait. All night. Just sit in a stairwell while trying to not look creepy as residents come home. Trying to not look creepy only makes you look creepier.

At about 4:00AM I literally say out loud: "Elohim Elohim Sabachthani" (my God, my God, why have you forsaken me?)

That's what Jesus cried out on the cross as he was dying. I cried it out while sitting in a staircase in

Williamsburg. It felt the same at the time. I felt so abandoned, alone and betrayed. BUT THEN. Day broke. 5:00AM rolled around and I felt at peace. I made it through the night. I survived. I could make it in this city. Everything would be okay. I kept waiting.

At about 9:00AM my sister-in-law's friend texted: "Hey, just woke up, sorry!"

SHE WAS INSIDE THE APARTMENT SLEEPING THE WHOLE TIME.

Look. Sometimes people will disappoint you and you'll feel alone. But it won't last. And you're not alone. Sometimes you just have to sit in a stairwell through the night until the day breaks.

Keep hoping and keep persevering.

My First Job in NYC

Let me preface. I moved to NYC without already having a job. Just some money in savings and hope. I came to the city to pursue comedy but needed to make money. No idea what I was doing.

One of my dad's business contacts set up a job for me at a super fancy Italian restaurant in Astoria. It's still there. Trattoria L'Incontro. The manager Vinny still runs the place. Very suave guy. I've never worked in food before so this felt like going straight to the major league without having never swung a bat. FEELING REAL CONFIDENT.

It's January and snowing. I'm from Florida. I'm numb but not from the cold. I take two hours to get to Astoria even though it's a 45 minute ride. I get off the train and immediately walk into the Trattoria restaurant. I walk to the back and announce to a very large Italian cook that I'm Paul, and I'm here for my job.

"What?"

"Paul, I'm here to be a busboy."

"Who?"

"Is this Trattoria L'Incontro?"

"NO. No, no. Down the street."

Did you know that there are 7.9 million restaurants in NYC that begin with "Trattoria". Haha. What a hoot. So hilarious. No clue. Currently fighting back tears. About to walk into a new job with puffy eyes.

I finally find the RIGHT Trattoria. I'm covered in snow and panic. I'm greeted by one of the smoothest, sharpest men I've ever met in NYC (I've met about 3 people so far including the burly man at the mistaken Trattoria). He's very kind. He can tell I'm tense. I had the vibe of frantic-parent-searching-for-lost-child.

"You okay."

"Me? Yes. Yes? Sorry I'm late, I'm so--"

"Take a breath. It's okay. Take it easy."

Day one, already crushing it. Nailing the first impression. Vinny shows me around the restaurant and introduces me to the staff. Another bus boy takes over and shows me the ropes. I don't remember anything.

I went to college for 4 years and graduated Cum Laude. Everything is going over my head. Real intense stuff like, how to place the table cloth and when to refill waters. He tries to show me how to make an espresso. HAHAHAHAHAHAHAHA. No. It's so impossibly complicated to me that I don't even bother trying to learn. I will quit before I ever have to make one solo.

"You got it?"

"Yes, absolutely."

I survive my first day. I'm convinced bus boys should be making six-figure salaries.

Day two. I get there on time. Vinny is VERY
impressed. I'm hanging on by a thread. Work begins and
I almost feel like I know what I'm doing. ALMOST (I
don't actually). I'm filling up glasses of water,
replenishing bread for the table. Totally crushing it as
NYC's newest bus boy of the year. I change a table cloth
BY MYSELF.

Immediately break a pepper shaker.

My soul leaves my body. Abandons my physical
being. Bye, you deal with it, idiot. I'm in a panic
grabbing handfuls of pepper with my bare hands.
Another bus boy cleans it up like an adult. Vinny
reassures me. Vinny's reassurance makes me want to call
him dad. I keep my head low the rest of the day.

Day three. I show up on time. Again, Vinny is VERY
impressed. Or surprised. I can't tell. Greet Vinny and let
him know that I'm quitting. He acts shocked. Asks me if
I'm okay. We both laugh on the inside. I think about
hugging him but don't. He hands me an envelope of
cash. As I walk to the subway I check the envelope. $80.
I'm rich. Oh no, why did I quit? Two days of work and a

broken pepper shaker and I get $80? $80 is way too much money for what I'd done. Or rather what I didn't do.

I got another job that week. God showed me pity. One involving zero pepper shakers.

Whatever you're struggling through. Give it more than three days. Give it a week and then one more day. You can overcome it and conquer it. Just think, if I had persisted and kept working hard I would've been able to accomplish incredible things like: setting a table. Cleaning a table. Not break pepper shakers. But I still never would've learned to make an espresso.

My Worst Job in NYC

When I moved to NYC I was willing to do anything for money. I mean. Not ANYTHING, anything. But pretty close. My first couple years in NYC were rough. Lots of crying. LOTS of crying. My first place I found on Craigslist. It was a windowless room with a curtain for a door in an apartment without a kitchen or living room in a 5-story walk-up. I paid $860/month and slept in my sleeping bag. My roommate was a Romanian guy that would sometimes peek in my curtain to see if I was home.

I was living like a king.

It was winter and raining a lot but luckily I managed to get an outdoor job. Praise God. Ticket taker for NYC Airporter. It's a shuttle service that buses people from the city to the airports.

This job opened my eyes to the brokenness of humanity. The depravity of souls. The raging sin that perches on the hearts of man. There's something about taking a bus to the airport that INFURIATES people. It's not like a school field trip. It's more like a prison bus taking you to be locked up. No one is happy.

My spot was right outside Grand Central. I'd work 12 hour shifts. Standing outside in the cold.
My shift routine was as follows:
-Get on the bus
-Check each person's ticket
-Get cussed at by people who couldn't get a seat
-Create a line of angry people on the sidewalk to wait for the next bus
-Get cussed at more
-Rinse. Repeat. 12 hours.

For lunch breaks I'd eat McDonalds and sit on the floor somewhere inside Grand Central. To this day there are corners and nooks inside Grand Central that I look at and think: "ah, yes, my old lunch spot."

I worked right outside this restaurant called Pershing Square. I'd stare in there for hours at the people eating and drinking, fantasizing about having enough money to eat there. One day I would sit in one of those booths and look out.

One day as I was throwing myself a pity-party, stalker-staring into Pershing Square I had my worst interaction with a customer. Little boy Paul was about to be destroyed:

It's late in the night. The guys selling tickets don't care if there's a bus already there waiting or twenty minutes away. They're selling tickets and telling people, "there's a bus! now give me your money." Then I get to deal with the angry people.

A bus just pulled away. A woman rushes up to me. Visibly furious. This lady has screamed "let me speak to the manager" countless times in her days.

"WHERE. IS. THE. BUS?"

"Sorry, ma'am, you'll have to wait for the next bus."

"NO. I need to be on the bus right now."

"... But there's no bus right now. You'll ha--"

"ARE YOU F***ING KIDDING ME?"

"No ma'am. I apologize, there's no bus right now."

(It is very hard to hide a bus. I'm not David Copperfield. What's she waiting for me to be like, "hah, kidding! here's the bus, right behind your ear!")

"NOW I'M GOING TO BE LATE. YOU MADE ME MISS MY FLIGHT."

(Technically, her poor time management made her miss her flight. not me. I did not say this.)
"Ma'am, I'm sorry, there will be another bus--"

"THIS IS YOUR FAULT. F**K YOU. YOU MADE ME MISS MY FLIGHT. YOU'RE GOING TO HELL."

(That's a bit of a leap. But also. How hilarious would it be if she were right? What if in that moment I died, went

to Hell and Satan was there waiting like, "you know what you did.")

She storms away and grabs a cab. I'm shaky with adrenaline. Confrontation cripples me. It feels like I was just assaulted. All my innocence is gone. I want to cry. I do cry. I look over into Pershing Square. The warmth of the lights inside. The people without a care in the world. In that moment I promised myself to make enough money to one day eat in Pershing Square.

~Fast forward seven years~

I'm married with a baby. I've had a rollercoaster of different jobs, but now I'm stable(ish). I get to do stand-up. I've made a lot of friends. This is practically a different universe from the one when I first moved to NYC.

To celebrate seven years in the city my wife took me to Pershing Square. The host sat us in the exact booth I'd always stare at. Finally, I was inside the warmth looking out at the cold. Staring at the spot where I used to stand.

As I sat across the table from the love of my life and precious baby boy, all I could think was:

"WOW this place is overpriced. Terrible food."

Enjoy the little treats in life my friends.

Preparing for Fatherhood

(It's July, 2018. In two months I'm going to be a dad, so I'm reading a baby book.)

Our OB recommended a parenting book to help us know what to expect each trimester. I'll be frank. It's mainly stats about how things go wrong, why things go wrong, ways to not kill your baby, and fun anecdotes about how impossible it is to be a good parent. So I'm feeling good. I'm good. You're good? Good.

Reading through the book makes getting to a new trimester feel like I just beat a level in a video game. MISSION ACCOMPLISHED, BABY IS STILL ALIVE, NEXT LEVEL. What the book doesn't tell you is that the final level is birth and you're the boss that the baby defeats. Game over, new life has won. Then you read about more ways your baby can die and ways you'll probably screw up as a parent (especially you, dads, LOL). This is why they say making a baby is a miracle. Because there are a trillion things that can go wrong. And even when things go as planned there are still things that can and will go horribly awry.

We've also turned to other parents for advice. Other parents don't really give advice so much as they give warnings on two things:

1. Ways to not kill your baby
2. POOP WILL GET EVERYWHERE INCLUDING YOUR MOUTH

Multiple parents have informed me, "oh, you're having a boy? well he's going to pee in your mouth when you change his diaper." JACKPOT! The spoils of parenthood, amiright? I gag VERY easily. Can't wait to accidentally throw up on my precious baby boy.

Books and parents warn to help prepare you for the worst. It comes from a loving place. I'm genuinely thrilled and grateful that I get to be a dad. I just have to appreciate that there might be an increase in days where I wake up and think OH NO I HAVE NO IDEA WHAT I'M DOING. Then eat a sandwich and be fine.

My First Girlfriend

Honestly, I don't know if it even "technically" qualified as dating, but I still count it. I'm not going to use her real name in the story (close to her real name, but not her real name).

It was sixth grade. I had bright blonde hair and glasses. I was the fastest runner in sixth grader (something I'm still proud of). I wore glasses and tighty-whities. I was not confident. Whenever the teacher called on me to speak in class my face would get beet red, my eyes would water and voice would shake. Truly a PILLAR of a man.

I heard the "hot" girl had a crush on me. This is huge. This is life changing. I already see us getting married and me doing badass things like speaking in class. As one does in sixth grade, I was told this steaming, hot piece of intel through a series of her friends passed along to my friends. Very reliable.

"Becky has a crush on you. You gonna ask her out?"

"I guess."

"Oh dude, you like her, don't you!"

<face turns bright red and I start sweating>

"We're going to tell her you like her too!"

Time slows down. I lose all focus on school. It feels like a grenade just went off by my ear. A girl is going to know that I, Paul Schissler, HAVE A CRUSH ON HER. All sounds are muffled. I'm floating in a dark sea. No idea what we're learning in class the rest of the day. School is pointless. Education meaningless. Only thinking about my future girlfriend.

By the way. I forgot to mention earlier. I HAVE NEVER SPOKEN WITH BECKY BEFORE. We saw each other in school occasionally and our friends took care of the rest.

I put together a game plan. My body put together a nervous stomach ache. Perfect. In between switching classes, I planned to run up to her, ask her out, she would say yes, then BOOYAH. Dating.

Bell rings. All my dumb friends watch me make a beeline for Becky. I'm sweating. VERY bad stomach ache. Face deep red. I reach Becky. This is it. I lay my heart on the line like a knight in shining armor.

"Hi"

"Hi"

"Will you be my girlfriend?"

"Yea"
[then immediately walks away]

BOOM. Welcome to girlfriend town, chumps. Just like that I'm in a committed relationship. It takes the entire rest of the school day to come down from the adrenaline rush of talking to her. I, Paul Schissler, am a boyfriend.

We don't speak for the next seven days. We don't ever speak.

No idea what I'm doing. Too afraid to call her on the phone. Blowing it. Hard. James Blunt's "Goodbye My Lover" plays on constant loop in my head.

At the end of the week I get a voicemail on my home phone. You know, the home phone, where your entire family can listen.

[voice of a boy clearly impersonating a girl]
"Hey Paul, this is Becky, your girlfriend, are you going to call me on the phone or anything? hehehe."

Devastating. A prank call from a dumb boy IMPERSONATING MY GIRLFRIEND. I should fight for her honor. I do nothing.

The following Monday her friends tell me she wants to break up. Totally get it. Honestly, really wise move on her part. One of the cornerstones of dating someone is communication. One of the cornerstones of communication is actual communication.

I am incredibly relieved. And incredibly single.

If I could tell my sixth grade self one thing about dating: don't be afraid to talk to people. Eventually you will talk to people, make friends and you'll meet your dream woman and get married.

The First Time Meeting My In-laws

Quick preface: I'm white. My wife, Esther, is Korean. The week leading up to meeting my future in-laws, my wife's friends prepared me. Just kidding. They TERRIFIED ME. It was like an episode of that prison show "Scared Straight" where inmates shout at troubled youths to keep them out of jail. So like that, but with meeting Korean parents.

"Korean culture isn't like white people. It's not all laid back and chill."

"DON'T touch her in front of her parents. No hand holding, hugging, kissing. NOTHING."

"When you're at dinner, don't drink or eat ANYTHING until her father begins."

"Again, NO hand holding or touching their daughter."

"It's best to speak as little as possible. Actually, don't talk. Sit there and smile and don't say anything dumb."

Needless to say, I was confidently looking forward to a pleasant dinner with my then-girlfriend's parents.

Her parents are in town on a trip for her Father's church. Her dad's a pastor. I'm actively thinking of scripture to slip into conversation. It's the day of. Tonight I will meet my girlfriend's parents. I spent all week practicing "hello" in Korean. I butcher it perfectly. I decide to work remotely out of Esther's office that day. It makes me feel less anxious to be close, plus we can leave together to meet her parents at the restaurant. Perfect.

Esther gets a call from her mom that they're near her office and want to stop by to say hello. Perfect. PERFECT. PERFECT. NOT part of the plan. No. I'm not ready to meet them yet. Abort. Abort. Should I hide in the bathroom stall? I'm not mentally ready yet.

I instantly start sweating. The nervous poop monster pops up in my belly. My face is turning red for no reason. My hands start shaking. Why are my hands shaking? Stop shaking. Esther asks me if I'm okay to meet her parents.

"Hah, totally, babe. of course. yes. absolutely fine."

I lie.

She looks nervous too for some reason. Oh no. Why is she nervous? Oh God. She knows I'm going to blow it. We're both nervous. I keep wiping sweat from my hands and doing my best impression of "guy who knows how to breathe properly."

Her parents walk around the corner. Eagle has landed. You got this white boy. All my "scared straight" training comes flooding in. I walk awkwardly fast toward them. Slow down what are you doing? I reason it's polite to walk to them before they walk to me. This is the woman I love's parents. This is a big moment. I need to make a good first impression. Esther's mom is visibly aware that I'm visibly VERY nervous. It's surreal to see someone absorb your energy and reflect how badly you're freaking out.

She says hello. I say hello in Korean. Offensively bad. Her smile is like a hug. She skips a handshake and hugs me. She holds my hand and keeps patting it and smiling at me. She doesn't let go of my hand. That's how visibly nervous I was. She was consoling me like I was a trauma victim. She asks about my mom. Esther's dad smiles and says hello with a hearty chuckle. He doesn't speak again. A man of few words.

I hug her mom goodbye. I begin regaining consciousness. I feel so loved and accepted. So grateful for her parent's warmth. So laid back and gracious. Nothing like what Esther's friends had warned me.

We had dinner that evening and it was lovely. I followed all the rules: NO TOUCHING. Lots of sitting silently and smiling. At the end of the night Esther's father gave me a pen from his church. It felt like I was receiving a sword from the king. That was our conversation. Him giving me a pen. It was beautiful.

The lesson I learned was that you should take as much advice as you can from others who know better than you, but be confident in yourself. Trust who you are. And most importantly NO PDA in front of parents.

My First Time Doing Stand-up

Some people are just born natural stand-up comedians. I was not one of those people. I was born funny, but not born a stand-up comedian. Very different. It's taken a lot of work and even more failure. I still fail a lot, but I'm better at it now.

It was the day after my 21st birthday. I promised myself that when I turned 21 and was old enough to drink that I'd get on stage and do stand-up. I was TERRIFIED of public speaking. Just thinking about speaking in front of a crowd used to make me panic. So, duh, just throw a couple drinks in to get loosey-goosey. Booze confidence. I was living in Nashville for the summer. I Googled open mics in Nashville. Found a sports bar off the highway hosting an open mic. Tonight was the night. I didn't tell any of my friends I was going to do a mic. This was a solo journey.

I spent all day writing up a very crappy five minutes of "material." It was bad. Not even actual jokes. Knowing I would need a drink before even walking into the bar, I prepare a mixed drink. Tequila and grape juice. I put it in a water bottle. Grape juice was all I had. I didn't know better.

The drive to the open mic is silent. No music. No talking to myself. Silence. Fear. Doubt. Turn around. Nervous stomach ache. Oh no. Oh no. Oh no. I'm alone in my car driving and my heart is already racing. I pull into the sports bar. It looks much sketchier than I anticipated. Why would they have comedy in a place like this? They will hate me here. I am not "highway sports bar" guy. I'm "let's hang out at youth group" guy. I sit in silence in my car debating if I should leave. 10 minutes pass. I stay. Chug the entire water bottle of tequila juice. Gag. Alcohol is gross but WOW do I feel confident enough to leave my car.

When I walk inside the bar I immediately want to leave. Is smoking still legal inside bars? People are smoking. The people playing pool look like they are physical growths from this establishment. They are sports bar people. I ask the bartender if the open mic is happening. She points me to a large bearded guy. He's very nice.

"Hi, I'm here for the open mic? I'm Paul?" (I'm so nervous my own name is a question)

"Yeah man, just write your name down."

"Okay, great. Thank you. How long have you been doing comedy? What's it like?"

"Umm...I dunno, a few years. It's kinda just the same guys telling jokes around here."

"Wow. That's so cool. It's my first time."

"Okay. Well, you'll be okay. Just stand up there and do your thing."

"Thank you so much for having me. I'm so nervous."

"Okay."

Good work, tequila. Thanks for having my back and helping me nail that first impression with lots of confidence and coolness YOU IDIOT.

I sit down by myself. Observe the other comics. They're all friends. One guy is with his girlfriend. He looks cool. Mainly because the other guys look like they do not have girlfriends. The host starts the mic and announces the winner of the mic is awarded a free Fresca. I have never desired a Fresca more in my life. Don't even like Fresca. But winning a Fresca for being the funniest person in the room? I will die for that Fresca.

One by one, the regulars do their sets. They laugh for each other. I am confused. This is not the stand-up I've seen on TV. I don't know what this is. A couple are really funny. I'm hopped up on adrenaline and tequila so I laugh generously. The girlfriend guy does his set. He crushes. I follow.

"The next comic, it's his first time doing stand-up. Give him a warm welcome."

"Hi I'm Paul. Thank you..."

[everything is a blur]

A mix of cringe-worthy act-outs and shouting ensues. Other than that, no idea what I said. But I got some laughs. It honestly might've been two or three laughs. But they were real laughs.

It's over. I did it. So much adrenaline. I return to my seat and down a beer. The mic ends and the host announces the winner of the Fresca. In my head I'm making plans for my Fresca trophy. I'll put it on my mantle. Maybe I'll frame it one day and talk about how I won it at my first open mic.

The dude with the girlfriend won.

Makes sense. Good choice. He drank the Fresca. I'm dumbfounded he didn't want to keep it as a trophy. To each their own. I walk over to congratulate him.

"You were so funny, how did you do that?" (it was like a child talking to a magician)

"Oh, thanks, I've been doing it a few years. It was your first time? You were funny. My girlfriend was cracking up at one of your bits."
[I'm transported to heaven]

"Really? I mean, really. Wow, thank you. That means so much." [relax, Paul]

They thought I was funny. Someone other than my mom thought I was funny. I'll never stop doing this. I'll never come back to this highway sports bar, but I'll find other bars. Then shows. Then who knows! (Adrenaline was still surging through my veins)

That was it. That's when I was hooked. At a highway sports bar in Nashville, TN.

Nine Days Out From Being a Dad

a;lksjdfl;hasdjghsal;knf;lkashdkg!!!!!!!!!!!!

My wife's due date is in nine days. September 26th. I've heard from a lot of parents that the baby rarely comes on the actual due date. But it's about nine days. SO MANY EMOTIONS. Laughing while cry-humming writing this.

Family and friends have been incredibly generous. That means each day I carry boxes, packages and envelopes of baby stuff for the baby upstairs to our apartment. My existence is box carrier, to opener to box disposer. Repeat. So much stuff. At this point it makes more sense for me to throw out our bed, couch, table and just use diaper stacks as their replacement.

I'm so excited to be a dad. I'm so terrified to be a dad. I made a bucket list in my head of things to do before the boy comes. I didn't mean to. My brain instinctively did it. I'm not dying. Why would I do that? It's a death of one stage of my life, but it's more so a birth of a new stage.

My bucket list:
-sit in silence for prolonged periods of time
-sleep in
-sleep
-eat at restaurants
-take 20 minute showers
-sleep
-not smell poop

Frivolous things.

Our hospital bag is packed. Can you bring a beer in a hospital bag? Hah! J/K! (it's a bottle of Soju). Overall I feel pretty useless throughout pregnancy. Esther carries the weight and endures torture on her body. I buy ice-cream bars and chips. That is the cross I bear for this family. Walking to CVS for junk food. Paul: The Provider.

But we are a team. A unit. Creating life together has made us closer. I will love this boy, but not as much as I love his mother. His mom is awesome. I've never met him before, I don't know him yet. When he's born I'll tell you all his name. OR if you wire me $100k we will name him whatever you want. Even if it's dumb like Baby McBabyface. Or Sir Screech Da Baller. Or Chet.

Now that he's born, I can let you all know that his name is Owen. You're still welcome to wire me $100k even though you didn't get to contribute to his name.

The Day My Son was Born

Wednesday. September 26th. The due date. Not even born and our boy is punctual.

Today's supposed to be the day. This could be it. My wife and I both work from home JUST IN CASE. Everyone tells us that your first is always late so we're not too concerned.

Her water breaks. We think. Did it break? It's not like the movies where there's a waterfall and all of a sudden we're jumping out the window into an ambulance and some George Clooney-looking doctor is screaming "PUSH, PUSH" five minutes later. It was all very chill. I leave the house to drop off some paperwork at my wife's office. Then I go to the gym. This could be my last workout in a long time, and I want to be crazy buff for my son so one day he can say "my dad can beat up your dad" and all the other kids will be like "yeah, for sure."

So I'm in the gym, getting huge, thinking about how life is going to change forever and my wife texts me.

Wife: I'm getting contractions

Me: Should I come home?

Wife: Yes

Why would I ask if I should come home? OF COURSE I SHOULD RUN HOME IMMEDIATELY. I drop the weights (RIP to getting buff) and run out of the gym. Get on the Q train and almost immediately they announce uptown service is shut down due to an emergency. *$%&#@!!!!!!!. Of course. I'm freaking out. I sprint to the street to get a car. It's raining so traffic is extra bad. I manage to get a car but it takes FOREVER to make it home in the traffic.

Finally get home. We grab our hospital bags and jump in a car to the hospital. This is it. It's go time. It's really happening. How is it happening already? Nine months is a long time but how are the nine months already done? The boy is fully cooked and ready to come out of the oven.

The pregnancy waiting room is PACKED with pregnant women. NICE. PERFECT. Eeeeeeeeeverybody just feels like giving birth today, huh? There isn't any seating left, so they have us sit in the hallway. Yes. Pregnant woman having contractions, running a fever. Let's have her sit in the hallway. That's right. Wife was also running a fever that morning. BEAUTIFUL.

We sit in the hallway for two hours.
Fever.
Contractions.
Hospital hallway.
(Don't worry, they gave her a styrofoam cup of water.)

Finally we get her into a room. She's already past 5cm dilated. Lots of pain. They can't give her the epidural because the fever and contraction pains is giving her high blood pressure. At this point I've ground my teeth down all the way to the gums.

9cm dilated. No epidural. LOTTA PAIN. Luckily for my wife, she has me standing by her side:

"You okay?"
"It's okay."
"It will be okay."
"Okay?"
Just knocking it out of the park with words of encouragement.

She's endured up to 9cm dilated with zero pain medication before they finally give her the epidural. Thank God.

It's game time. Doctor says she's 10cm so it's time to push. No time to grab an extra nurse to assist.

"Paul, grab a leg"

I'm too jacked up on adrenaline to process thoughts so I follow orders like a scared 18-year-old in bootcamp. The "PUSH" part of the delivery was totally like the movies. Doctor and nurse shouting at my wife like coaches yelling from the sideline at their star player.

"PUSH, PUSH, PUSH, GOOD, YOU GOT IT, GOOD, GOOD, YOU'RE DOING GREAT, KEEP IT UP."

"HARDER! PUSH HARDER! YOU'RE ALMOST THERE!"

In a nearly inaudible voice I was saying, "good job, babe, good job." I haven't been trained in baby delivery shouting so I was A LITTLE SHEEPISH OKAY? It took her under 30 minutes to push him out. My wife is a bonafide, rockstar, champion of a badass. BAM. Pushed him out. I cut the cord with almost no difficulty, so we each contributed fairly equally.

The second I heard Owen Taeun Schissler cry his first cry I felt every cell in my body change. Melt. Burst with love. Explode with unrestrained joy. He's here. Our boy is alive and here and his cry is the most beautiful thing I've ever heard. In that moment I felt I would do anything for this person. I'll never stop loving him. I want to sacrifice for him, for this family more than I ever conceived of sacrificing.

Owen didn't ask to be brought into this world, but I'm thankful he's here. I hope one day he's thankful he's here and realizes what a gift it is to be alive. I hope he's as in awe of his Umma as he should be.

My First Time on a Plane with My Baby

Let me start by first apologizing to any parent on past flights at whom I rolled my eyes, gave a nasty glare, a heavy sigh or asked God to smite for having a crying baby. At the time I had no baby. I could put on headphones and escape it. You, with your crying baby were trapped in a Hell at the mercy of a tyrant.

We're flying cross country to California. Owen's first flight and it's cross country. Go big or go home. A few weeks prior we took him on his first road trip. He was a champ and slept most of the way. We're feeling confident. Borderline cocky. He's a natural born traveler. These are all lies we're telling ourselves. Babies have pacifiers, parents have lies they tell themselves.

He sleeps the entire Uber ride to the airport. Feeling. Real. Confident. We get through security with ease. He smells like poop. He always smells like poop because he's always pooping. Even when he just finished pooping he's already pooping again. It's his 'eau de parfum'. We wait to change him. Esther goes to the bathroom to pump milk. I feed him. Halfway through feeding it feels like he's sweating. He runs hot. His sweat is on my shirt. I lift him up. Oh, thank God, he didn't sweat on my shirt it's just HIS POOP JUICE THAT LEAKED THROUGH HIS DIAPER, ONESIE AND SWADDLE. Diarrhea on my favorite shirt. Such a gift.

Esther returns. She's tired. I'm tired. Owen is ready. To. Party. I take him to the men's room to change his diaper. This is my first time changing him in a public bathroom. I'm scared but confident. Look at me, I'm a cool dad wearing skinny jeans and a hoodie. I got this.

I did not "got this".

The second I lay him down on the cold, plastic changing table Owen starts wailing. WAILING. Huge tears streaming down his face. He's crying harder than when he got his shots. I'm in a panic. Someone wiggles the door handle to the bathroom. DO YOU NOT HEAR THE BANSHEE SCREAMING INSIDE, SIR?

The harder he cries, the more I panic. There's so much poop. I must push onward. I wipe. I cuss out loud. It's okay he's a baby he doesn't understand, Lord please forgive me. I cuss a lot more but quieter (sort of). I successfully change his diaper. I change his poop-decorate onesie with a new one. That really pisses him off. I gather him up and leave the bathroom. I'm sweating profusely. Owen hates me. I pass him off to Esther. Zip up my hoodie to cover the poop juice on my shirt.

If it's this brutal before we even get on the plane, what Hell awaits us in 26 D and E? I pray a mother or grandma is our seatmate. No dice. Large, middle-aged Middle Eastern guy. There are four other babies on the plane. In my heart I vow to earn trillions of dollars so we can take private jets everywhere in the future. We're terrified for the six hour flight ahead of us. No food, no headphones for movies, no books. Just holding a ticking-time-bomb-baby for six hours.

Miraculously, Owen is pretty chill. We feed him. He poops. It smells. Our seat mate is sleeping. Did the diaper fumes knock him unconscious? Maybe. We hold our stinky, poopy-diaper-filled boy for three hours. No movement. I can't feel my shoulder or either legs. The pain is worth not stirring the baby. Finally, we decide we need to change his diaper. There's a lot of turbulence. Seatbelt sign is on. Screw it, we gotta go for the bathroom. The steward saw us coming.

"Excuse me, you two really need to be seated there's a lot of turbulence right now."

OH REALLY I DIDN'T NOTICE THE PLANE JOLTING UP AND DOWN, SHOULD WE WIPE BABY POOP ON THE SEATS INSTEAD YOU MONSTER?

But instead I confidently say, "Sorry?"

Esther changes the diaper. I return to the seat cursing scientists for not already creating teleportation or some Harry Potter magical transportation.

Mother and son return. He's calm. The four other babies on the flight are flipping their sh*t. Our baby is calm. I feel so smug. Even as I hold my baby, I roll my eyes at the other parents with their crying babies. Owen sleeps the rest of the flight. We survived. The six hour flight felt like eighteen hours, but we survived.

I'm so relieved. So elated. This must be what it feels like to win an Olympic medal or climb Mount Everest and live. Life is all about celebrating the little victories. So like, loving, selfless parents, we celebrate by getting In-N-Out burgers before changing our boy's diaper.

First Time Pooping My Pants in 3rd Grade

Let me start by saying, I
HAAAAAAAAAAAAAATE pooping in public. Always
have. The thought of strangers waiting on me to finish
up so they can use the bathroom gives me a nervous
stomach ache. Then I have to go all over again. Also,
germs.

Mobile, AL. Pauline O'Rourke Elementary School.
I'm waiting for my mom to pick me up from school,
hanging out in the library with one of my best friends.
It's after school so we have the whole library at our
disposal. Bean bags, books and a stomach brewing up a
storm in one little blonde boy.

We're having fun. It's during drawing cartoons that I
feel the first rumble. Level 1. No worries, I'm sure mom

will come by the time I need to go poop. We keep drawing, laughing, being free like we're going to live forever.

We're running playing tag. I'm stopped in my tracks by the rumble. Level 2. I lose tag and don't care. Start assessing exit strategies. You might not make it before mom comes.

"Hey, let's take a break, I have to go pee."

I lie. I can't let my friend know I have to poop. Pee is a safe, respectable body relief. We find a faculty bathroom. It smells of pee. We turn on the light and see the urine smell is coming from the massive pool of urine surrounding the toilet. Classic. I can't use the pee covered throne. I gag but play it off like I'm laughing and run away quickly.

We keep playing. I'm in hell. Level 3.

We're throwing a ball back and forth. I fart. My friend smells it.
"Ewww, did you just fart"

YES THOMAS I JUST FARTED PLEASE FOR THE LOVE OF GOD GET OFF MY BACK I'M BARELY CLENCHING IT TOGETHER HERE.

(That's what I wanted to say)

"Haha, yeah, I tooted."

As I'm throwing the ball back it happens. Level 4.

It's not a fart.

It's not a shart.

It's not a rose-smelling heart.

Full on regular turds. Fills my whitey-tighties to the brim. He throws the ball back, I miss it. I can't bend down to pick it up because that will mash it all over my butt. I do what I can only refer to as the "bend and snap" (reference "Legally Blonde"), where my legs are straight and I slowly bend down on one side to pick it up, straightening up quickly.

"Ewww, what's that smell? Did you fart again?"

NO THOMAS THAT'S POOP I JUST TOOK A DUMP IN MY KHAKIS WHY CAN'T YOU JUST PRETEND TO NOT SMELL ANYTHING AND THROW THE DAMN BALL

"Haha, yeah, I tooted again."

[a few minutes pass]

"Did you fart again?"

"Yea, I did. I keep tooting, that's why it's smelling."

MOM WHERE THE HELL ARE YOU?

Just then my mom pulls up in her van. I grab my backpack and waddle-run out. You ever see a penguin try to run fast? That was me. Were I a wiser boy, I wouldn't have sat down when I got into the van. I sat down. Smoosh. The poop is no longer contained in my whitey-tighties.

"Mommy, I pooped my pants."

Miraculous Healing in a Wheelchair

Sophomore year of high school I was in a wheelchair for six weeks. I was a tall, lanky kid. Constantly growing. Very weak hips. Zero flexibility. To this day it's painful stretching to touch my toes.

It happened at soccer conditioning. You know that hellish period before you can even try out for a team? Lots of running, drills, getting yelled at-- all to eventually probably get cut. I'd never played soccer before, but my friends were doing it and according to my mom I did sports for friends. I had already quit football and swore I wouldn't do basketball again. It was nothing personal, I just didn't like any of the other players, coaches, sport itself and lacked the skill.

I ran really fast. Terrible at kicking a ball. Speed was all I had. I avoided the ball at all costs. That's not what you're supposed to do. Avoiding the ball in soccer is just cross country. Why am I here at soccer instead of cross country? Oh right, friends. We're playing a scrimmage and I'm sprinting as fast as I can. Just a blur of pasty white legs. I hear a loud *POP*

I fall.

I feel the *POP* noise.

I cry.

Just kidding. Crying happens later. Must look macho in front of all the guys so I do what every macho teen boy does who's in pain:

"Dude, dude, oh man, duuuuude. I don't know. My hip. Oh dude."

"You okay, Paul?"

"My hip. It hurts. Dude, this sucks."

Praying my mom will magically appear and fly me away on angel wings. Everyone thinks I'm fine and resumes playing soccer while I lay in the grass.

Can't move my leg.
Can't stand up.
I army-crawl to the sideline (Ok, so part of the way I roll like a log, but it looks cool).

I call my uncle to pick me up. He lifts me up into his van as "You Raise Me Up" by Josh Groban plays in my head. Now I cry like a little boy. Family vans are a home away from home.

MRI scans show that my hip flexor pulled away from the bone with a little piece of the bone. NOICE. Wheelchair for six weeks. No cast, just wheelchair. That's a big detail. Wheelchair with a cast on people go, "oh, he got in an accident." No cast, people stare. "What's wrong with that guy?"

I'm mature and wise beyond my years for a high school boy so naturally I fantasize about getting pity attention from hot girls at school. (Author's note: this never happened).

At school no one really cares that I'm in a wheelchair. Sort of looks like I'm playing a twisted prank on the whole school because I'm doing wheelies, carrying on as normal, no cast. No one cares. Except one kid.

My mom takes me to the library one day before school. A kid walks in rocking frosted tips, cargo shorts and flip flops (quintessential Florida). Already a bad sign. He makes a beeline to me and mom. This isn't good. I know this kid. He goes to the ultra charismatic church in town where everyone claims to speak in tongues.

"I'm going to heal you."

Boom. Right to the point. All business. I look at my mom. My mom is wide-eyed. She's the most God-loving, genuine Christ-like Christian I know and even she's got the what-the-hell-is-this look on her face.

"Is it okay if I heal you?"

WHAT ARE YOU TAKING MY ORDER AT A DRIVE-THRU?

"God told me to heal you."

God did not send me the same memo that morning.

The librarians are looking over. I feel very uncomfortable. I'm a Christian. I believe in healing and the power of God. But I do not believe frosted-tips in cargo shorts was sent by God to heal me in this high school library.

I agree to the healing. I take an order of "Miracle."

He places his hand on my shoulder and stresses that in order for it to work I need to believe. I want to wheelie on this dude so bad and roll away. BUT WHAT IF, RIGHT? The curiosity of some cargo short wearing kid actually healing me is killing me.

He prays out loud. Something like: "God, heal Paul's hip and make him walk. By the power of God, you are healed. Stand up."

I keep sitting because I don't know if he's finished with his miracle or still cookin'.

"Okay, now stand up."

"But I can't stand up."

He looks annoyed.

"You are healed. Now, stand up."

"I can't stand up."

"Will you just try standing up, please?"

I try standing up but can't BECAUSE MY HIP MUSCLE ISN'T ATTACHED TO MY HIP BONE. I try, then fall back into my wheelchair.

His response: "You didn't have enough faith."

THEN WALKS AWAY. My mom assures me it's not because I don't have enough faith. Doctors heal people too, not just teenagers in flip flops and cargo shorts. Stay healthy and stretch your hips, folks!

Trick-or-treating After My Grandpa's Funeral

It's Halloween and this is my most memorable Halloween story. Don't worry, it's not sad. I mean, it is sad, but it's also funny.

October 26, 1994 my grandpa passed away from diabetes. He was a great man. A person of character. Someone who brought levity to heaviness. My mom always said I got my sense of humor from him. I was four when he died so I don't remember much. Just his smile.

Equally heartbreaking was we would miss trick-or-treating because we had to go down to Florida for grandpa's funeral. They don't hand out candy at funerals.

The funeral landed on the night of trick-or-treating. I am a HUGE candy addict. Any money given to me goes straight to candy. This is a terrible year. I lose my grandpa AND a night of free candy.

It's an open casket funeral. I peak. Grandpa's wearing a stylish powder blue suit. There's grandpa. Laying in his casket forever. I'm fully convinced I see him move. I run to tell mom.

"Mom, grandpa moved!"

THAT MUST HAVE BEEN DEVASTATING FOR MY MOM. Your imaginative four year old telling you that your deceased father is moving in his casket. LOTS OF TEARS. (It's funny how kids can be so aware and yet not fully understand the reality of a situation. The weight. The pain. We know we feel sad, but we can't yet appreciate the depth of the loss that actually happened. That's why we have no filter on our imaginations and do things like tell our grieving mothers what we *hoped* we saw.)

The family returns to grandma's house. It's quiet. Adults are tired. All I can think about are the kids in costumes outside going door to door getting all the candy. One of those houses has to have Milky Ways. I can feel it. Mom, dad, aunt, uncle and grandma feel bad for the kids. They just had their first funeral and it's Halloween. They agree taking us out to get candy will cheer us up. They right. They ask us if we want to go. I'm not proud of being the first one to say yes, but here we are.

We have no costumes. You can't collect candy from neighbors in regular clothes.

ding-dong

"Trick or treat!"

"Happy Hallow-- sorry, what are you supposed to be?"

"Oh, we're a grieving family. Give us candy."
It's not a good look.

We decide to rummage the closets. Closets in grandparents homes are the best. Old toys, vintage clothes, haunted dolls. It's slim pickings for children halloween costumes though. One of the cousins wore an old dress, another cousin wore a frilly hat. Brother wore a an old man blazer and sister wore a sweater (I'm not 100% this is accurate because I was four, but it was something along these lines). I wear my grandpa's leather vest that had a hand-engraved horse on the back and one of his straw cowboy hats. And my velcro shoes. I was a cowboy. No clue what the other kids decided they were in their outfits. Librarian? Old man? 'Little House on the Prairie' cast member?

We use pillowcases for candy bags. First house is a neighbor friend. They're sorry for our loss. LOTS OF CANDY. Second house is sorry for our loss. They let us take handfuls. Every house is the same. Even if they didn't know we just came from a funeral, they open the door and see this rag-tag, tired family with kids dressed in old people's clothes and pity us. Sweet, sweet pity. This is the light in the darkness.

The "costumes" are itchy and we have our pillowcases filled with candy. We've only been trick-or-treating for six houses but we all want to go home. One too many kids dressed as the grim reaper or a skeleton feels like one of those dark, twisted "ooh too soon?" jokes.

I have a pile of candy. My sweet tooth is throbbing. I'm aching for a Milky Way. I remember grandpa died from diabetes.

Though not entirely sure, I know it has to do with sugar being bad. Sweets are bad. I'm torn. Candy makes me happy. Will it kill me? Will it make my family sad?

I'm four. I eat the Milky Way. And Smarties. Then only like two Three Musketeers, another Milky Way, Skittles and a Jolly Rancher. Okay, fine. Then I finish with a Tootsie Pop.

I'm a kid. I live in the moment. I'm happy. I'm sad. I'm crying. I'm laughing. I miss my grandpa and would trade all the Milky Ways in the world for him to be back. But I can't. I can eat my candy. I can be with my family.

And I can proudly wear my new leather vest that has a hand-engraved horse on the back.

Love you grandpa.

Brotherly Love

Brothers fight. It's in our DNA. We love each other, but we don't have the emotional development to express our love in words so we punch each other instead.

"I'm beating you up to make you tougher" = "I love you"

One day in high school my brother and I were in the middle of a match to see who could show each other the most love AKA full on rage throwing basketballs at one another.

My brother is two years older and plays football. I am a beanpole of boy. My arm doesn't have the same strength and accuracy as my brother. Thankfully I am lanky and quick, making me a harder target to hit. Like all of our fights I have no idea how or why we started fighting. All I know is that it started civilly:

"You're an idiot"

"Shut up, idiot"

"NO YOU SHUT UP YOU IDIOT"

"YOU'RE AN IDIOT, YOU IDIOT"

We ran out of words to exchange so we picked up basketballs. Getting pegged by a basketball hard enough will make you stop talking.

Bro hits me hard in the leg. I black out into Hulk-level rage. He turns his back for a split second. In true younger brother form, I go for the cheap shot and launch a basketball in the middle of his back. For a millisecond the joy of victory floods my body. That millisecond does not last. We both stop and stare at each other.

Time freezes.

We both know I'm dead.

I'm not angry anymore. I am hopeless and terrified.

Everything is in slow motion. I do what I do best as a younger brother in a fight with his older brother.

I run.

I sprint inside the house. I can hear my three-sport-playing athlete brother's footsteps close behind. Those speed drills at practice have been paying off for him.

I'm in a panic. Need to hide. They say the safest place in a house to hide for shelter during a hurricane or tornado is the bathtub. I run to the bathroom. Jump in the bathtub. Assume the fetal position.

As if he's working renovations on a construction site, my brother takes my body and shoves me into the tiled wall.

CRUNCH

We freeze and lock eyes. Together we slowly back away and see a fetal-Paul-shaped indentation in the wall.

Now this next moment is critical. Every sibling knows whoever calls out "MOM" first is innocent.

He beats me to it.

"MOM, Paul busted a hole in the bathroom wall!"

The audacity. Oh, I busted the hole in the wall?!?!?! I WAS YOUR RENOVATION TOOL. Mom runs in and grounds us both immediately. For our punishment we have to fix the bathtub wall.

The bad news is that we had to renovate the bathtub. The good news is that we learned to renovate a bathtub.

I learned two valuable lessons that day: run faster and always be the first one to call mom.

Call your mom today (or mom-figure, Aunt, grandma). Pick up the phone and give her a ring.

Psychological Warfare With My Sister

My sister is the eldest. I'm the youngest. We were usually allies against my brother. There's a bit of a motherly-son vibe with older sisters and baby brothers. We all had our roles in the family. Megan the cruise director. John the protector. I was the jester. I was there to diffuse tension and make everyone laugh. But sometimes the jester fights back. We all love each other but we also all fought each other. Family love.

We're at our family cabin in the Georgia mountains on vacation. This cabin is the most special place in the world. Built from the ground up by my grandpa. It's a haven of love. A home of warmth and joy. It's also where I once rage-cried over losing a game of UNO.

The cabin is small. Tight quarters with siblings for prolonged periods of time is a breeding ground for fights. Any little thing to scratch that pent-up-aggression itch.

No idea why we started arguing. Megan probably beat me in a game of Scrabble and I went berserk (that word would've got me so many points). This isn't supposed to happen. I'm supposed to fight with my brother and get saved by my older sister. Not tonight. Bedtime at the cabin had a storm brewing.

Brother fights are simple. Shouting and name calling. Physical altercation. It's done. Eat a snack together.

Fights with sisters belong in a psychological thriller movie. My sister knows how I tick. All my weaknesses. Weaknesses I don't even know I have. The only weakness of hers that I know of is that she pronounces bagel as "baa-gul". Sisters implement their intelligence in fights. They conquer. Baby brothers get emotional and cry to mom.

My sister knows I gag easily. VERY easily.

One time I took too big of a bite of a bread roll and it made me throw up. Just smelling urine makes me gag. Writing about this is making me gag.

Megan and I are at the peak of our shouting match. Mom is telling us to stop. Like respectful, loving children, we disregard and escalate things. We run upstairs to fight without pleas from our mom. This is the final battle. No turning back. No apologies now. My sister plays my weakness.

She hocks a huge loogie on my shirt.

I didn't know she had it in her.

This is my nightmare. It flies over in slow motion. I'm so shocked she spit that I don't actually believe it happened.

Slowly, like I'm peeking under the bed to check for the boogey monster, I look down on my shirt.

MASSIVE LOOGIE.

I puke immediately.

Megan's victorious laughter stops abruptly upon seeing me puke. She return-pukes.

Brother and sister puking together. An eye for an eye, a puke for a puke. Sometimes your weakness becomes your opponent's weakness. We're both crying and shouting. There's vomit everywhere. Mom runs upstairs and sees the aftermath of our battle.

"WHAT ARE YOU TWO DOING? GO CLEAN UP RIGHT NOW, YOU'RE BOTH GROUNDED!"

I've never been grounded for throwing up before but I totally get it. Fair call.

We got over that fight and forgave each other. We still laugh about it. But to this day, my sister can fake the sound of making a loogie and I gag.

JOKE BREAK! (Stories will resume after this brief message of jokes)

People are a lot less judgy when you say you ate an "avocado salad" instead of a bowl of guacamole.

My favorite part of eating healthy is the junk food I eat immediately after.

Kudos to boneless wings for convincing everyone they're not actually chicken nuggets.

My favorite part of a salad is when it's finally over.

Gang initiation: Eat tortilla chips when you have a cut on the roof of your mouth.

Putting a napkin on my lap at a sad hotel continental breakfast feels like wearing a tuxedo to a barn dance.

People are A LOT less judgy when you tell them you ate "potatoes and chicken" instead of chicken nuggets and fries.

I didn't eat "leftover pizza" for breakfast. I had tomato and cheese triangle toast.

I have a lot of self control when it comes to eating. Like, even when I don't want to finish a pizza I'll force myself to eat the whole thing.

The only cardio I do is when I eat my food really fast and get out of breath.

My First Patriots Game

If you're a Patriots fan, cool. If you're not a Patriots fan, still keep reading. When you get married, your partner's loves now become your loves. My family loves Auburn University football. So my wife became a fan. My wife's family loves the Patriots. So I'm a fan. When her parents moved to the states from Korea, they came to Boston. A family's NFL team allegiance is a big deal in American culture. Boston was their first American home. The Patriots were their team all the way.

My father-in-law had never been to a game before. Like a good son, my bro-in-law wanted to make his dad's dream come true. He got him tickets to the season opening game. My wife and I invited ourselves along.

Game day. We drive from NYC to CT to pick up the bro, then on to Boston. I'm behind the wheel, going over the speed limit to impress my bro-in-law. Pick up my wife's dad from the airport. Everyone's excited.

Traffic on the way to the game is of emergency-evacuation-of-a-city level chaos. Luckily we manage to snag a $17,894 parking spot. Walking to the stadium is like trying to weave through a riot of drunk zombies. Game hasn't even started and the drunk shouting going on is, well, worrisome. I don't care for loud, drunk crowds. They're unpredictable and scary.

We make it into the stadium. Hordes of people. It's a diverse mix of large, older white men that have guts rivaling a 9-months pregnant belly, and backwards-cap bros who are one "WOOOO" from setting a most-consecutive-WOOOO's-in-a-row record. And there's us.

This stadium. This crowd. Is huge. Crowds, loud music, drunk people-- all of it makes me want to curl up in a quiet attic with a book. Needless to say, I'm having a blast. Smiling big to convince my wife I'm having a good time. She knows I'm not.

We buy a couple beers for $851. Total steal. My bro and father-in-law have seats in a different section. We part ways. We find our seats. Awesome, the two seats next to me are empty. Maybe we'll have some extra space.

Two WOOOO bros sit down next to me.

"WOOO! HELL YEAH, BRO! LET'S GO PATS!"

"Hey, sounds good. Alright."

"WOOOO"

"Heh, wooo, yeah."

I'm hitting it off with the bros splendidly.

They're both very drunk. I look at my wife and smile. She mouths "sorry".

WOOOO Bro #1 leans over to me like we're close enough for me to be the best man at his wedding.

"DON'T YOU LOVE THIS, BRO?"

"Sure do! Actually, this is my first Patriots game."

I can tell his entire world goes into slow motion. The stadium is outer space silent. He's having an out-of-body-experience. This is a spiritual moment for him. He takes off his hat. Lowers his voice and gets serious.

"Are you serious, bro?"

"Yeah. First time."

"I'm going to take good care of you and make sure you have an awesome first game."

"Thanks so mu--"

"You're gonna be the bigGEST PATS FAN BY THE END OF THIS GAME, BRO."

It was a beautiful crescendo of passion.

I turn to my wife. My smile is quivering.

Bro #1 turns to Bro #2. He whispers with that loud, drunk person whisper that everyone can actually hear.

"Bro, I swear to God. When he said it was his first Patriots game, I got a f***ing tear in my eye. I feel like I'm his dad."

This is now the best, first Patriots game ever. I just got adopted by a Pats bro. Like a good father he offers me beer. Like a good son, I decline.

Every time the Pats score a point or make a good play, my Bro Father hugs me vigorously, shakes me, and/ or high-fives with enough force to be considered assault. At this point I'm rooting against the Patriots so I can have a few minutes of relief from my Bro Father's celebration-battery.

It's finally third quarter. I don't know from what energy source Bro #1 and Bro #2 draw their energy, but it's endless. The WOOO's don't stop. They only increase with alcohol. Their shouting is beginning to annoy other Pats fans behind us. They engage cordially.

"HEY YOU TWO, SHUT THE F**K UP"

"What the hell, we're on the same team, man"
Bro #1's feelings are hurt.

"TAKE YOU AND YOUR LITTLE FA***T BOYFRIEND OUTTA HERE"

Bro #1 is angry.

"YO, F**K YOU. WE'RE BOTH ON THE PATS. I'LL F**K YOU UP."

The Pats fans all around us start booing my Bro Fathers. As their son, I'm humiliated. My wife and I crouch farther away from them.

Two police officers approach the Bros. The fans start cheering. No one cares about the game anymore. The police officers tell the Bros to come with them. Before leaving, my Bro Father turns to me in all of his drunken-loving-weary splendor.

[shrugs his shoulders and shakes his head]

"I'm sorry, bro. Sorry about all this. Enjoy your first game."

Now I almost teared up.

"It's okay, fath-- I mean, bro. Hope you guys are okay."

Bro Father smiles.

"Go Pats."

"Yeah, Go Pats."

Then the cops escort him away to stadium drunk jail.

I don't remember who won that day. What happened during the game. Or even who the Pats played. But I'll never forget my first Pats Bro Father who took me under his wing at my first Patriots game.

My Son's Baptism

We got our baby baptized. It's not as crazy as it sounds. All that happens is you hold your baby underwater for six minutes then parade around the church with sparklers while the pastor sings a Christian rock song. Standard stuff.

Actually, baby baptism is about us, as parents, making a public commitment to raise our child in/ with the love of Jesus with the support of our church community. Maybe that sounds crazier to you? That's okay. It was a special day. Here we go.

Baptism day. We're having Esther's dad baptize Owen. Super special. Esther's dad is the pastor of a Korean church in California. We've been staying with her parents for the whole month of December while Esther's on maternity leave. Owen is an immediate celebrity with all the older church members. Pastor's daughter's son. MAJOR CELEBRITY.

Due to his high profile in the Korean church community, we want to make sure Owen is dressed devastatingly cute. We forgot to bring the white gown that I wore for my baby baptism so we opt for corduroys, flannel shirt, suspenders and bowtie. Total hipster. But the clothes are all tiny and baby-like so it's cute.

Before church we have to pick up rice cakes (in Korean it's called "dduk") for the post baptism feast. We're new parents and don't have a grip on life because babies are impossible, so we're running late. Perfect. We're late to our own son's baptism. Esther's mom texts her to let her know that we're late to our own son's baptism. Feeling good! Thanks for the reminder!

There's a baby in the car, so I drive a safe 48 mph over the speed limit. The desire to not disappoint my mother-in-law far outweighs my fear of God's wrath for being late to church.

We're flying down the highway. Just as Esther and I are discussing how Owen hasn't pooped yet this morning we hear an explosion. Sounds like someone dropped a pipe bomb in a tunnel. I look to see if any cars around me are in flames. Nothing. I look in the rearview mirror.

Esther is wide-eyed.

Owen is grinning.

The smell is strong. Potent. Ruins the interior of the car.

Diarrhea explosion.

We can't check because we're in a moving car, but we know it's bad. We pull into the church parking lot. Nice. We made it! We're only 42 minutes late. WHEW! Thankfully, we collectively smell like baby poop. We take Owen out of the car seat.

Oh no.

It's bad.

It's worse than we thought. I don't really understand physics, but it turns out, if you're sitting on your baby butt in a car seat, and you get explosive diarrhea, it will shoot upward, downward, outward and beyond. It will Jackson Pollock paint your clothes with feces.

It went through his diaper.

Through his flannel onesie.
(flannel is thick material)

Through his corduroy pants.
(VERY thick material)

Through his swaddle blanket.

Oh. Baby poop is yellow. His clothes are now stained yellow. We could play it off as mustard stains, but answering the question "why were you spreading mustard on your son's butt?" is way more embarrassing than the reality.

We wipe him and his clothes down with 237 wet wipes. It's almost helpful.
It's baptism time.

We take a seat in the front pew. I'm holding our crime-scene-looking child. My arm and hands are strategically covering his butt and back area.

ALSO. This is a Korean church so I have no idea what's being said. Esther's father motions for us to come up on stage. He asks us a few questions in Korean. We both say "yes" in Korean (it's one of the few words I know). Esther's father makes a comment about me saying "yes" in Korean. The whole church laughs. HAHAHA. Classic white dude burn.

Joke's on him because I'm about to hand over a smelly, poop-covered diaper. Hopefully he's generous with the holy water. The only thing that can possibly cleanse this boy of the sin that covers his body and clothes, is holy water.

I hand-off the baby to my father-in-law. I look like the world's politest quarterback handing off a football made of eggshells. He sprinkles a few drops of water on Owen's head. Says a few things in Korean. Seems like he's speaking faster than usual. That stench is hitting him.

Baptized. Boom. Righteous baby.

He passes Owen back. Catching a whiff of the poo I almost instinctively pass him back. Like a game of hot potato. Service ends. We made it. Oh wait, SIKE. Now we get to eat and mingle with all the church members.

Grandmas swarm Owen. They can't get over how cute he is. His cheeks need to be pinched. We put him in his stroller. No one is picking him up. There's no way we're going to let someone pick him up and have his cute-baby-celeb-status tarnished. Can't come back next year and hear:

"Aw, how's your poop baby doing?"

He stays in the stroller. We eat fast and get out of there.

We did it. We hid the mess and got the boy baptized.

We're in the car, pulling away from church and--

EXPLOSION

I look in the rearview mirror. Esther's eyes are closed and she's clenching her jaw.

Owen laughs.

Remember folks, always carry around wet wipes and an extra outfit!

A Tribute to My Mom and Dad for Their Birthday

My parents have the same birthday. January 22nd. When I was a little kid, I thought that all parents had the same birthday. I figured that when two people got married they both agree on one last name and one birthday. Shake hands. Settled. Marriage.

I wasn't alone though. My older brother thought that you had to FIND someone who shared your birthday to marry.

Can you imagine how much more of a HELL dating would be if that were true?

"So, what do you look for in a girlfriend?"

"Oh, you know, a really sexy June 13th."

But he's my older brother so I believe everything he says. Older brothers' word is law. Fact. Commandment. I immediately Googled which celebrities had my birthday. June 13th. The Olsen twins!

Jackpot. I'm going to marry twins (I did not. Thank God.)

The First Time I Heard My Mom Cuss

Before I begin, allow me to make it 100% clear that my mom is a living angel. The most patient of patient people. Selfless. Loving. Slow to wrath. Quick to forgive. Boundless grace.

But human.

I'm somewhere between the age of 4-6. Momma is wrangling my sister, brother and myself to go somewhere. Ever my mother's plight-- rounding us up to get somewhere on time. Just. Get. In. The. Van. Now.

We all pile in our huge Chevy Astro (we had a picture of an angel on the front plate and named the van "Grace"). Doors close. We're going to make it on time.
Mom freezes. She's not holding any keys. She exhales a beefy sigh. One of those long sighs that you've

stored up for an entire week. She forgot the keys inside the house. Mom runs to the house to grab the keys. She freezes with her hand on the door. Another long, beefy sigh. The sigh of an entire month.

The door is locked.

The three of us kids unload and check the back door and the basement door.

Locked.

This isn't good and we're definitely going to be late. Tension is building as we sit in the van like it's our raft in the middle of an ocean. We wait for mom's game plan. She's standing by the driver side door, head in hand. Doing the slow back and forth head shake trying to muster up words to even mutter words. She's tired. Stressed. Frustrated. Then she says it. The three of us kids hear my mom say a bad word for the first time in our lives. (BRACE YOURSELF).

"Crap!"

The three of us freeze and lock eyes. I'm holding my breath. I'm exploding with fear and confusion internally. My world is shattered.

MOM JUST CUSSED. DOES THIS MEAN THAT I GET TO SAY CRAP NOW?

Bad words were not permitted in our house. Couldn't say "that sucks" or "shut up". We couldn't even watch 'The Smurfs' (because of witchcraft). Hearing "crap" was mind-blowing for three goody-tushu kids.

One of us instinctively calls out, "oooooo, you said a bad word."

My mom, the saint, immediately gushes an apology for uttering such an offensively crass word in front of her innocent children. We graciously offer forgiveness. And lots of giggling. As we convene on the side of Grace, my brother volunteers to climb a ladder and crawl through an open window. Success. He gets the keys, we pile in and drive off. Late to where we're going. As a family.

The Time Dad and I Got Killed in Laser Tag

My dad used to work at this laser tag place called Q-ZAR. It was huge in the 90s. When your dad works at a laser tag place you get to play free laser tag. Cha-ching! Dad always found a way to get the hook up for fun things like laser tag, amusement parks, buffets. You know, the true joys in a kid's life.

We're at Q-ZAR for one of my siblings birthday parties. Everyone is psyched. Hyping each other up to shoot each other with lasers. There's candy, cake and soda to make sure all the kids become berserk killing machines.

I'm young and small. The laser tag vest is too big and the gun is too heavy. I'm terrified. All the other kids are older and seem disturbingly prepared for combat. The laser tag instructor is preparing us for battle. All rules and guidelines are sure to be thrown out the window the second we're released.

My dad is behind me the whole time. I'm small enough to stand between his legs. He's calm because he's an adult and knows this is a fun game. I'm a shivering chihuahua. This is my Vietnam.

The laser instructor brings us into the battle zone. It's dark with strobe lights and deafening 90s techno. This is a nightmare house for a boy who enjoys drawing cartoons and sunshine.

The alarm rings and battle begins.

I'm shot with a laser almost before the alarm finishes ringing. (I get it. Little kid = easy target.)

I run with my dad to a cove to avoid the crossfire. Kids are going absolutely bananas. They've been storing up this blood-thirsty energy since birth. They are all in full 'Lord of the Flies' mode.

By the fifth kid that jumped out of the darkness, screaming while lighting me up with his laser gun, I break down in tears. Dad whisks me away. To protect ourselves we crouch behind a steel oil drum. My back is to his chest and we're shooting at anything that moves. Father and son taking on the wrath of adolescent rage. I'm still crying.

A little boy casually walks up to us as we sit crouching behind the oil drum. He proceeds to rack up dozens of points shooting us point blank with his laser gun. We just kind of sit there and take it because we're crouching behind an oil drum. It's not even shooting fish in a barrel for this kid. It's shooting dead fish on the ground outside of a barrel.

But he's a kid and my dad's an adult. So my dad shoo's the kid away like he's a gnat. I had forgot. This is the real world kid, you have to shoo when an adult tells you to shoo. I have the most powerful weapon in this laser tag game. My dad.

We shoot him as he runs away. Dad picks me up and carries me out to the sunny lobby. Then, as grizzled, laser tag veterans do, we eat some cake.

My First Insecurities

Do you ever trace an insecurity back to a childhood memory? You know. For fun? Just brew in feelings of inadequacy?

Just me? Cool.

Throughout my life I've struggled with: not feeling smart (aka being "dumb"), the need to be liked, and physical flaws I can't change. Fun stuff!

I've traced each insecurity back to a moment in elementary school. There's probably other instances that fed into each insecurity but these are the ones I remember. This week I'll share about feeling dumb. The following two weeks I'll cover my need to be liked and physical flaws.

The First Time I Felt Dumb

First grade. I'm the youngest in my family and my older brother and older sister are extremely smart. Every teacher I have comments on how good of students my siblings were. I have to live up to their standard. I can't be the dumb Schissler that teachers gossip about:

"All the Schissler kids were excellen-- well, except Paul he ate sand."

Our elementary school in Mobile, AL had a gifted program. Brother and sister both took classes in the gifted program. It's my year to test. I'm so nervous. At first I'm excited because I was invited to take the gifted program entrance test. HUGE HONOR. (In reality I think all kids took it.) This was my chance though-- to separate myself from all the schmucks in regular class and join the brainy elite in an Alabama public school gifted program.

Oh no. What if they find out I'm a genius? Can they find that out in this test? Maybe it will just be obvious.

Wait. What if they find out I'm like really, really, dangerously stupid? After the test they'll probably put a helmet on me and stick me in a short bus.

Maybe I'm so low-key genius they'll mistake me for being dumb.

Or. Maybe they'll just know I'm dumb before I even take the test and they laugh at me.

I was brimming with confidence.

It's my turn. I take the long walk through the school hallways to an empty classroom. Just me and a gifted teacher.

She assures me there's nothing to worry about.
YEAH EXCEPT FOR MY ENTIRE FUTURE LADY.

We begin. She has me play with wooden blocks. I crush it. Next she has me look through a series of picture cards. I'm to give alternate names for each object.

Card one: [picture of a doorknob]

"Doorknob?"

"Yes, good. What are some other names you might call it?"

I.

Shut.

Down.

"Umm... door grabber?"

She smiles with the smile of a thousand reassuring mothers. Eyes of hope. I can feel her screaming answers telepathically. Sorry lady, my thick, dumb head can't hear you.

DOOR GRABBER? WHAT THE FIDDLESTICKS IS
A DOOR GRABBER THAT'S NOT A THING PAUL.
DOOR. GRABBER. GRAB-BER? NO. STOP. NO.

"I don't know."

I don't remember any of the rest of the test. All I
remember is not getting into the gifted program. From
then on I never thought of myself as one of the smart
kids. And WOW did I resent door grabbers.

I failed to get into the gifted program. I'm average
and dumb. I can't be smart. That's not my role. I'm one of
the dumb ones.

Lies.

I believed those lies for most of my education. But
just because I didn't get into some special program
doesn't mean I'm stupid (technically maybe it sort of
does). But that doesn't define me. Once I found the
things I was interested in learning I did well.

When I look back on that dumb gifted test, all I can think is:

DOOR HANDLE

First Time Getting Teased for the Name 'Paul'

I love the name Paul. It's my favorite first name that I have. But no matter how much you love your name, little kids will find a way to make fun of it. No name is safe. Even if you didn't have a name, children would mock your no-name name.

Peak name-mockery season of life was the first grade. Everyone is learning words and getting real cocky. Why use education for good when you can eviscerate your peers' names?

I wanted to be liked. By everyone. I was nice to all the other kids, shared well and paid attention in class. In my mind, I'm safe from getting teased because who the hell teases the nice kid?

Kids.

That's who teases the nice kid. Kids because they're kids. The first time I was name-roasted caught me off guard.

A few girls approach me on the playground. Very pleasant. Smiling. Smiling too much. TOO MUCH SMILING IS BAD. Smiling turns to giggling. GIGGLING IS VERY, VERY BAD.

"Hey... Polly Pocket!"

[girls in unison]
"HEHEHEHEHE... POLLY POCKET"

I roundhouse kick all three girls at the same time. They burst into flames and disappear.

I wish.

My face turns beet red. In that instant, I envision the Polly Pocket that my sister owns. I've only touched it a few times. I don't play with it though. I'm not a Polly

Pocket boy. There's no way they could know I've played with it once, twice, maybe six times.

"Hey, Polly Pocket, do you have a Polly Pocket?"

[UPROARIOUS GIGGLING]

"No I don't. I'm not Polly Pocket. I'm Paul."

Stupid girls. My name isn't even spelled the same. If it was 'Pauly Pocket', okay fine. I see your case. But we're talking P-o-l-l-y versus P-a-u-l.

Doesn't matter.

In retaliation I do what every self-respecting kid does in this type of situation.

I run.

They chase me for twenty minutes shouting "POLLY POCKET". But I learned a valuable lesson that day: Polly Pockets are evil.

The boys played a different name-game.

Another day of first grade. Another afternoon on the playground. Another day of minding my own business digging in the sand. One of the boys from class walks up on me.

"Hey, Paul."

"Hi."
(sweet! making friends)

"Paulie wanna cracker?"

(BURN IN HELL YOU SOULLESS MONSTER)
"No, I don't want a cracker."

"C'mon, Paulie wanna cracker? HEHEHE."

"NO. I'm not a parrot. I don't want a cracker."

The more I say I don't want a cracker, the more he asks if I want a cracker. Children are cruelly persistent creatures.

The truth is, I would've loved a cracker. Crackers are delicious. Any cracker. But I couldn't fall into this demon child's trap of name games.

I was so hurt. Why would someone make fun of my name. That was the first time I felt insecure and self-conscious about my name. PAUL IS A NAME FROM THE BIBLE. The audacity. The blasphemy.

I cried about it to my mom. My mother is a peacemaker. She would never suggest revenge. She would never be like, "his name is Ryan? Then call him 'Lyin Ryan' because he's a little liar who smells." She would never offer awesome, vengeful advice like that.

My mom told me to take the high road. Next time some kid says, "Paulie wanna cracker?" I should respond, "No, I want the whole box."
That blew. my. mind.

GENIUS. They wouldn't see it coming.

I was so hyped up. In my room pacing back and forth repeating "NO, I WANT THE WHOLE BOX, SUCKA," like I was getting ready for a rap battle.

Next day on the playground I was AMPED. On high alert for little punk 'Lyin Ryan'. Like clockwork, he walks up to me by the sandbox.

"Hey, Paulie wanna cracker?"

Adrenaline surges through my body. The excitement of getting to use my retort is euphoric. Like I just ate a handful of sour straws all at once and the sugar punched me in the brain and tickled my tongue. I let him have it.

"NO. I WANT THE WHOLE BOX."

It feels so good. I wait for him to bow at my feet. He stands there with a confused look on his face.

"So... you *do*? Paulie *does* wanna cracker?"

SONOFA--

"Hah, Paulie wants a cracker! Paulie wants a cracker! Paulie wants a cracker!"

I'm deflated. Once again, totally owned by my peers. And once again, as a self-respecting, honorable first grader, I do what I do best. I run. He chases me, shouting, "Paulie wanna cracker?"

I hate parrots.

I wish I had a happy ending for you. Like, ten years later Lyin Ryan was attacked and killed by a flock of parrots. But to be honest, he's probably doing really well. Good job, good family. And who knows, maybe he even named one of his kids Paul.

We all have different names and that's beautiful. I hope you love your name and celebrate names of new people.

Love,
Paulie "Wants a Cracker" Pocket

The First Time Someone Made Fun of My Body

Every person I know has at least one insecurity about their body. Even people who are models. Physically perfect people. We all have mirrors, an attention to detail and a hefty supply of self-loathing. We are humans. I'm fine with my body. Other than the things I hate about it, it's fine. It's a good soul-transporter here on Earth until it's time to depart for Heaven. Gets me from point A to point B.

Like with most insecurities, a benevolent stranger or friend brings it to your attention. Something about you struck their eye and they just NEEDED to let you know about that mole on your neck. That's how I found out I hate my left ear.

I'm in second grade. All the kids have to wait outside the school before the bell rings. That means all grades are intermingled before school starts. Older kids are scary because they're bigger, faster, stronger and they know that. They know that you know that. You're at their mercy.

As a kid I have no idea what I'm insecure about yet. I'm a kid. I want to play and eat candy. I'm not old enough to stare in the mirror for 45 minutes and Terminator-scan my body, square inch by square inch, fantasizing about what needs to be fixed. Those joyous moments come in middle school. I'm a second grader. I don't even care if I wipe my butt properly yet.

I'm waiting in line to enter the school near my friends. Quietly. Dreading going into school. I would like school, but numbers and math exist. So I hate it. Out of the corner of my eye I see a large kid walking towards me. He's massive. Goliath proportions. He must be a third grader. Hell, maybe even... a fourth grader. My heart races.

"Hey kid."

(he refers to me as "kid" because he, being at least one grade older than me is CLEARLY the adult. I, a mere child.)

"Um, hi?"

"What's up with your ear. It's all pointy."

"What?"

"Yeah, your ear is pointed. It looks like an elf ear. Are you an elf?"

(my face is ON FIRE RED. my soul left my body to search for a new vehicle. humiliated about this p.o.s. second grade transport)

"No I'm not."

"It is. Is your other ear pointed?"
He checks my other ear.

"Oh, it's just your left ear that's pointed."

THEN HE WALKS AWAY.

Wow. Had no idea the spawn of Satan's son attended my elementary school. Such a true honor. He trained him well in the art of subtle destruction.

I reach up and feel both ears. I'm angry because he's right. How did this Lord of the Rings Rivendell-looking ear go unnoticed until now? That kid's eyes are as sharp as this dumb ear.

I try to adjust my bowl cut to cover the tip of my point. As far as I'm concerned 100 school kids are staring at my ear right now. Every giggle I hear I'm certain is directed at me. They must know too. Damn it. Now everyone is going to call me "Elf Boy".

The bowl cut does nothing to help me hide the ear. The rest of the day I spend casually holding my hand over my ear. Very smooth. Either the move worked or none of my classmates care because we're in second grade sniffing flavored markers. I'm staring at everyone's ears. Like I have some weird, non-sexual ear fetish.

Rounded top. Rounded top. Rounded top. Those lucky bastards. They have no idea how good they have it.

When I get home from school I want answers. I confront my mom about the deformity sticking out of the side of my head trying to pass as a human ear. Why would you allow this? Why did God make me like this?

You and dad don't have pointed ears. No one else does. Why me? Can we fix it? Use a system of tape, glue and string to unfold the top to round it out?

She tells me I'm made the way I was supposed to be made. How my ear is, is perfect the way it is. There's nothing wrong with it. In fact, it's special because it's unlike everyone else's ear. It's unique.

I felt okay about my elf ear. My special ear. It's not that bad. Honestly, I feel worse for that kid who made fun of me. He only has two boring, round ears. Lame, normal ears. Poor guy.

Whatever your insecurity is, I hope you try to look at it differently. It's not a flaw, it's a special touch. It's an artistic touch on your body.

Take it from an elf, you look good the way you are.

The First Time Meeting My Wife

I honestly don't even remember it.

She remembers it clearly and remembers thinking to herself, "wow, that guy is so rude. So full of himself."

Truly love at first sight.

Here's what happened: she was walking in Central Park with one of her friends with whom I went to college. They ran into me hanging out with "some blonde girl" (my wife's words). Apparently I chatted with my friend from college but COMPLETELY IGNORED MY WIFE (her words).

The second time we met (the first time I remember) was at coffee hour after church. If you're single and attend church, coffee hour is that special time after service where you can get a free cup of coffee, mini-muffins and stare at your crush from across the room but not go up to her because you're a coward and she probably has some finance boyfriend anyway.

Great place to mingle.

At coffee hour one Sunday I ran into my college friend and her friend (MY WIFE). This time we actually talked. This interaction I *do* remember and not because my wife is watching me type this. I distinctly remember this interaction because I remember how uplifted I felt after talking with her. She's like a powerlifter of lifting others up and making them feel good about themselves. Feel good about life. She radiates positivity. But real positivity, not like a smiling, programmed robot you'd see in a Christian theme park. She was open and inquisitive. Laughed easy. Smiled a lot. Genuine smiling like she knew who she was and was happy with it. You believe in yourself more after talking with her. She appreciates you without needing to know your backstory and what you have to offer. I felt like I could succeed in life. Run a marathon. Write a book. Go vegetarian for an entire day. Life-changing feelings.

It was an impressionable two minute chat.

"Wow", I thought, "what an amazing person."

"An amazing person who I have no interest in dating."

"It's great that now I'm friends with an older girl at church who's a counselor. She'll be great to talk through all my girl problems with."

THOSE WERE MY REAL THOUGHTS.

These were my wife's real thoughts about me:

"That boy needs Jesus."

"That poor, young comedian boy needs help."

"Oh boy, he needs community. He's lost."

"He's actually a nice kid. Much nicer than that jerk I met in the park."

"I should try setting him up with some single gals at church."

We were friends for two years. Platonic friends. Zero attraction or interest in dating each other. She's six years older so I wasn't even on her radar as a potential mate. She would constantly try to set me up with her single friends or suggest women at church to date. I would lament about my dating woes, she would talk about her dates. Anytime we met up for dinner or coffee she would pay. Because I'm a "poor comedian boy who needs help."

It was a great friendship.

After being friends for about two years, something changed. The scales were lifted from my eyes. She took me out to dinner for my birthday. She looked really hot. I remember shoveling sushi rolls into my mouth, not able to concentrate on what she was saying because she looked GOOD. And smelled good. Her whole essence was sexy. I wore a backpack to dinner and didn't shower that day.

I happened to be dating a woman at the time who was a year older than her. I thought, "well clearly an age gap isn't an issue with me, so why haven't I ever tried dating Esther?" (Things were clearly going really well with the woman I was dating).

Then I felt mad at Esther. She always tried setting me up with her friends, but why hadn't she ever set me up with herself? How dare she not fall madly in love with me. How could she NOT be falling head over heels for this $20k/year-earning-aspiring-comedian, who still shared a bedroom with another adult? Obviously I was a prime candidate for a successful church counselor who had her own bedroom and 401k.

Eventually me and the other woman broke up. I met up with my sexy platonic friend to talk through the breakup. Get her wisdom and consolation. I was really, REALLY, hoping for consolation. Like, arm around my shoulder, hug-it-out, consolation. From my platonic friend. My hot, platonic friend.

Our dinners became more frequent. I even paid for one. A couple months later we were dating.
SO. You know that really good friend you have, who you're like "Pfff, I could never date them, we're like best friends. It'd be weird."

Try dating.

Worst case scenario, it doesn't work out, things end terribly, the friendship is ruined and one of you has to move to Alaska to work an oil rig. Life goes on. But at least you gave it a shot. Best case scenario, no one moves to Alaska to work an oil rig.

Asking for My Wife's Hand in Marriage

We decided that during our summer trip to her parent's in San Diego that I'd have a talk with them. *THE* talk.

Just a boy, standing in front of two traditional Korean parents, asking for their eldest daughter's hand in marriage.

We've been dating about nine months. We know we want to get married. Not just so we can have sex because we're both saving ourselves (I promise)((Seriously, I promise))(((I PROMISE))). It's important for me to have a face-to-face conversation with her mom and dad about marrying their daughter. I can't do it over the phone. That's cowardly.

"Hi, it's me, Paul. The white guy who was just staying at your house for a week. So. Huge fan of your daughter. Love her. May I have your blessing to marry her?"

<phone hangs up>

It has to be in person. They need to see and feel my fear. My humility. Look into my soul and decide whether I'm worthy enough to spend a lifetime with their beautiful daughter.

I tell Esther I'm ready.

I'm not, but I say that I am. We both need to believe that I'm a strong pillar of a man who's ready to lead a family.

I'm ready to marry her. I'm less ready to meet with her parents solo. They speak English but are more comfortable speaking in Korean. I'm more comfortable speaking English because that's the only language I know. Esther always translates for us. This will be the first time we'll be talking without the comfort of our mutual buffer.

Like I'm cramming for the SAT, I start memorizing the Korean words for "love", "daughter" and "Please have mercy on me."

I'm the first white person anyone in the family has dated. I can't help but feel like I'm whitewashing a role in their family tree. There are already three strikes against me: I'm not Korean, I'm six years younger and I'm a comedian.

NOT. THE BEST. RESUMÉ.

Esther tells her mom that I want to take her and her father out for breakfast in the morning. Just the three of us. Her mom knows immediately what this is about. (This is all happening in Korean with me standing nearby like a man awaiting trial while attorneys talk). She says her mom said that if I'd like to talk about *that*, then we should all talk together.

"If you two are going to make a decision together, then you two need to come to Appa and I together."

WHEW. My lawyer will be at the trial.

The next morning we go to a hippie cafe. I say "hippie cafe" because it's run by hippies. There's a big tree in the middle of the restaurant and all of the employees have names that sound like they should be in 'Lord of the Rings'. We order coffee and pastries. MY HEART IS POUNDING. I keep counting down from 10 to nudge myself to start the conversation, but keep chickening out. "10, 9, 8, 7, 6, 5, 4, 3-- better start over, 10, 9, 8..." After about six minutes of doing that in my head while everyone does that thing where we silently smile at each other while fondling our coffee mugs, I launch into my spiel.

"I love your daughter, Esther, very much."
(AS IF I NEEDED TO CLARIFY WHICH DAUGHTER.)

The second I say "I love your daughter", her father's eyes start to mist and he looks away.

This is good.

I ramble a five minute speech about how she's the perfect woman, how I admire her so much, how she's the one I want to spend the rest of my life loving and serving, just like Christ served the church. It was so much more eloquent in my head. I was certain they would applaud.

There is no applause.

Her mom smiles kindly and nods her head. Oozing with love and grace she gives her rebuttal.

"Paul. Marriage is very hard. I want the best for Esther. I'm thankful that you are healthy and love the Lord. But. I am also a little concerned. How will you be able to provide for Esther and a family?"

In my head I'm like, "WOW. Me too. We're on the same page. And to provide for a family, I plan on marrying your daughter. She has a 401k and health insurance."

Before I could fumble a response my lawyer cuts in.

"Umma, I know the man that Paul is. He's a hard worker and will do whatever it takes to provide for his family. I trust him. I trust us to work together."

Dammit I love that woman.

Her parents nod.

"He co-founded a website and has a salary. The company could be worth a lot of money one day."

Parents nod more positively.

I look at Esther. We look at her parents. I don't know where this leaves us. Do they approve? ARE THEY GOING TO TELL ME *NO* AFTER I JUST PAID FOR PASTRIES?

"So?..."

"Yes, yes, you have our blessing. We are very happy for you both and love you both very much. So happy Esther will be getting married."

We all laugh, smile, cry and stop fondling our coffee mugs. What a relief. Thank. God. So happy. Now we can relax. Then Esther's mom goes:

"So. When is the wedding?"

The Proposal

After getting Esther's parent's blessing, things happened fast. It was the end of August.

Umma: "So. When is the wedding?"

Me and Esther: "Hahah. I know right? Oh, you're serious? Well, I mean, of course, the thing is, um, heh, uh, I mean, hah, probably definitely we were thinking like next summer-ish. Big ish?"

Umma: "Why wait so long?"

M & E: "Good point."

The parents talked with the grandparents. Esther's younger sister was engaged before us which we assumed meant they'd get married before us. Problematic. That's not the way things work. Life goes from eldest to youngest. Eldest married first, then middle, then youngest. It was grandfather's strong recommendation that we, oh, I don't know, not screw with the way familial marriage traditions have worked for thousands of years (my words, not his).

We weren't even engaged yet but we needed to be married first.

The wedding would be December 31st. New Year's Eve.

No ring.

No plans.

Three months to plan a wedding. Let's do this.

"We can do this. It's doable. This is going to happen. We got this." We told each other this every day. My "joke" about just bypassing the fanfare and going to the courthouse felt less like a joke each day we got closer to December.

It's September. We're deep into planning our wedding and I haven't even bought a ring yet. No idea what I'm doing. The only jewelry I've bought in my life was for my mom from a JC Penney catalogue. I text Esther's girlfriends and sister to find out what kind of ring she wants. I mean, I asked her what kind of ring she wanted, but you get a much more honest answer when her girlfriends read my texts to her, she tells them and they tell me. The system works.

I'm terrified of jewelry stores. I know nothing and they can tell. In my head I'm going to get hustled into buying a key ring with a pebble glued on top for $10,000. One of my best friends said he'd take me to his "ring guy". Had no idea people had jewelry "guys". I thought that was just an obviously fake thing in movies. My friend has now become my dad, taking his wide-eyed, fearful son into the jewelry store. His "guy" shows us some stones and bands. Every question he asks me, I instinctively look to my friend for fatherly guidance.

"Paul's looking for something a little more like this one. (whisper in dad's ear)

"With this cut of stone."

(whisper and giggle in dad's ear)

"And much smaller."

After much sweating I decide on a ring. (Full disclosure, Esther's friends texted me the exact ring she wanted so I knew what I was looking for. Open communication is key. She has to wear the thing, so why not know exactly what she wants to wear?)

I leave the jewelry store holding the ring in my pocket like I'm smuggling a priceless artifact out of the MET. The entire subway ride home I'm envisioning hypothetical fight scenarios where someone tries to rob me and I magically know how to all of a sudden kick ass. I get shot, but get the ring back. Esther is over-the-moon touched by my bravery and we fly off into the sunset in a hot air balloon. You get the idea.

It's now October. Our wedding is two months away and I STILL HAVEN'T PROPOSED YET.

Mid October I finally decide on the right day to propose. It's Saturday. I have an all-day class but can't pay attention because there's an engagement ring in my tote bag and immediately following the class I'm going to propose to the love of my life.

Esther meets me after class. I lie and say that we're going to meet one of my high school friends and his girlfriend in Central Park. Lying during the proposal period is crucial. A successful marriage is built on trust and lies during the proposal.

I have one of my friends wait in the bushes in the park with his camera to capture the moment. Probably not wise to have a buddy dressed in black, crouching in bushes at the park at night time. I mean, he could've been arrested or maced by a passerby. He's a good guy.

As we're walking into Central Park, and I fondle the ring box in my pocket, Esther stops.

"I just don't get why you haven't proposed yet. We haven't sent out invitations, or announced our engagement yet and we're only two months away from the wedding. You know what, maybe you don't even need to propose. Let's just announce the wedding so we can move forward."

MY HAND IS ON THE RING IN MY POCKET AND I'M LITERALLY MINUTES FROM PROPOSING.

I am exploding with rage inside. And joy. Because she is going to feel like a monster in about two minutes.

"Be patient, my love. I know it's frustrating, but I want it to be a special memory for us. Just trust me, please."

I crush it with the patient, wise boyfriend response even though secretly I do it to be self-righteous.

We get to the spot. My friend and his girlfriend are not there. Esther's confused. Not happy.

"What the heck? Where are they? It's cold and dark, and I'm hungry. Let's just go--"

I grab both her shoulders and look deep into her eyes.

"Esther. You know I love you very much. You're my person. With you, I'm home. Esther Youngshin, with you marry me?"

I get down on my knee and pop open the ring box. She starts crying.
"Yes, yes!"

She's bawling. We hug.

Later she told me she was crying, not from elation, but because she felt so guilty about arguing with me about not proposing.

My advice to anyone who wants to get married is: go to the courthouse and elope. Get a ring pop or wrap some wire around each other's fingers, and live your life. That's love.

A Honeymoon Disaster

We took our honeymoon six months after our wedding. Gave us a chance to save up some money because weddings are ungodly expensive. Plus it allowed us to settle into married life for a bit. Get used to each other as husband and wife before taking a long trip to a foreign land together.

We went to the French Alps, Lake Como and Turin, Italy. I've never been to Europe before. The closest I'd come to traveling internationally was visiting Epcot and eating at different "countries".

The months leading up to the honeymoon Esther is hyping up French food. Oh, the food. Oh, the amazing, delicious French food. Cheese and wine like you've never had in your life. I love cheese. I'm sold.

Once we land we get our rental car. We tell them it's our honeymoon and they upgrade us to a Mercedes Benz. Travel tip: always tell everyone you're on your honeymoon and they will give you free stuff. Even if you're traveling alone. They'll probably give you even more free stuff because of how pitiful it looks that you're honeymooning alone.

Our drive through the French alps to our AirBnB is beautiful. The whole time Esther's describing all the delicious French food we're going to gorge ourselves on. I'm salivating. We haven't eaten since our airplane meal. I'm starving. She doesn't let me stop at a McDonald's on the way because it'll ruin our appetite before enjoying an authentic, delicious French meal. My one chance to try French fries in France. Gone. French fries are authentic French food to me. That argument is quickly shot down.

We arrive to our quaint mountain village that we'll be staying at for the next few days. It's breathtaking. Straight from a postcard. A village nestled between majestic snow-covered mountains. We stroll around town to find something to eat. We're the only people walking around. It's a ghost town. So strange. Every shop is closed. Weird. Every restaurant, closed. WEIRD. I begin to panic. My love for food is almost as deep and wide as it is for my new wife. She planned this trip. Where has she taken us? Why would she take us to this haunted town in the alps? This food-forsaken village?

As her loving, patient, new husband, I begin to blame my wife. Where was all the delicious, French food we would be scarfing down? Sure this trip was to celebrate our union, but more importantly, WHAT ABOUT THE DAMN FOOD?

Day one of our honeymoon and I'm mad at my wife for a trip she planned, researched and organized all by herself while I complained.

True romance.

We discover that we are staying in a ski town. It's not ski season so everything is abandoned until winter. Perfect. For dinner on our first night of our European honeymoon we find a convenience store and buy some stale bread and cheese.

Day 2: For breakfast, lunch and dinner we eat bread and cheese.

Day 3: More bread and cheese.

Bread, cheese and wine is romantically French until it becomes the only sustenance available to survive.

Three days of eating mostly cheese. WE ARE THE MOST CONSTIPATED WE'VE EVER BEEN IN OUR LIVES.

On the fourth day we drive to the airport for Italy. On the way we stop by a super fancy restaurant. Finally, we'll be having one of those out-of-this-world, delicious French meals.

It. Is. Incredible. This was the amazing French food Esther had been hyping up for months.

Truly a perfect romantic dinner. A rich, 8-course meal with wine and complimentary champagne (we told them it was our honeymoon). I've never eaten such rich food in my life. It's especially rich compared to the three days of bread and cheese sitting in our bellies. Like an annoying college bro, I egg-on Esther to finish off the wine since I'm driving.

"It's expensive wine. Chug it!"

The roads out of the Alps are windy. Snake-like curves for hours. I feel like James Bond driving the Benz through the sunset mountains with my smoking-hot wife sitting in the passenger seat who's unusually quiet, swaying back and forth with her eyes closed. Oh God this isn't good.

"Honey, are you feeling okay?"

<silence><head shake>

"What's wrong?"

"I feel sick."

"Like throw up sick?"

"Yes."

"Like throw up right now, sick?"

"Drive slower."

James Bond is gone. Nervous husband Paul is back. Every curve we drive around is punishment to Esther's nausea. That damn rich food. If only we had eaten McDonalds instead, we wouldn't be in this mess.

It's almost midnight. We pull into town near the airport to fill up on gas. As I get out of the car to fill up, Esther also gets out.

"Babe, it's okay, I'll fill it u--"

She sprints to the dumpsters beside the gas station. I HEAR PUKE POURING OUT ON THE PAVEMENT. It sounds like buckets of soup being dumped out.

All I can think about is what a waste of half of a $400 dinner. And also, how sorry I am for my sick wife.

She walks back to the car like a zombie. She is in a daze of life-ending food poisoning. We drive to the airport to drop off the rental car before heading to our

AirBnB for the night. As I'm about to park the car, Esther gets out.

"Sweetheart, it's okay I can park it, you don't need to hel--"

She pukes up every ounce of life inside her body. This parking garage is now christened with once very expensive French food. I drop the car keys in the drop box. Esther is barely conscious from sickness. We jump in a cab and as we're about to tell the driver the address, Esther reaches in her purse and discovers she doesn't have her phone. All the information for our entire trip is in her phone. We make eye contact and watch all hope leave each other's eyes. We jump out of the cab and race back to the rental car.

I am in full take-care-of-your-wife mode. The inner provider, protector and partner is awakened within me. Esther, who has been leading us and taking care of us this whole trip is now out of commission. It's my turn. God help us.

I peer into the passenger side window of the rental car. Esther's phone is in the car door pocket.

"AL;KDS@&*@#%$$%$*!@^%%^@(*^@$*&HJIU H*&@#Y(*Y%(*@Y$T(*NIOF*(Y@(#YU$*($YT(*H OIFJ(*Y#@(U%()JJ@@$"

I bottle it up inside. Don't explode on your sick wife. Don't explode on your sick wife. Don't explode on your sick wife. She didn't do this on purpose. She's hanging on by a thread. Sick as a dog. I tell Esther I see the phone. The keys are locked in a drop box and there aren't any employees because it's past midnight.

"What should we do?" I ask her.
"Break the window."

I look for something heavy to break the window. I ALMOST COMMIT TO BREAKING THE WINDOW. Almost.

We decide against it. Instead we figure out a way to get to our AirBnB then come back early in the morning before our flight. Thanks to the kindness of a stranger letting us use his computer, we get the information for our AirBnB and get there around 3 AM. Esther continues to vomit. Thankfully, we are able to sleep for an entire 45 minutes before having to head back to the airport. Fully rested.

There are no employees at the rental car company early in the morning. At this point I am very anti-France. I denounce all things French (except French fries). This is how I'm repaid as an American after we helped them in World War I?!

I was a tad emotional.

We can't miss our flight to Italy. We call the rental company's customer service and tell them to hold onto the phone. Esther pukes the entire flight to Italy. We are swimming in romance. Two lovebirds blissfully enjoying a honeymoon.

We land in Italy. The sickness has finally subsided. The rental car people can't mail the phone to us. I tell Esther we can buy her a new phone once we're back in the States. We give up on the phone and drive to Lake

Como. Maybe it's a blessing in disguise-- not having the distraction of her cellphone so we can be present with each other. Once in Lake Como we get a call from the rental car company. They're holding onto the phone for us. Esther looks up Google Maps on my laptop.

"We could take an impromptu road trip."

"Where?"

"France."

"No. We just came from Fran--. No."

"It's only four and a half hours to drive back to France to pick up my phone."

"No. That's insane. We're not going to back track nine hours round trip to get your phone."

I put my foot down.

We drive nine hours round trip to pick up her phone.

And you know what? Everything worked out. We took a surprise road trip back through the Alps for a cellphone and enjoyed our time together. Just husband and wife, alone, figuring out the road bumps in life as a team. In sickness and in health. That was the point of this trip. To experience life together. To experience each other. To be in our own little world before going back to face the real world. Together. Forever. There will be more puking, crying, lost phones, and arguments over French fries. But there will be even more love, patience, and growth as one.

Thank you for being my wife, Esther.

Living with Three Women in a One Bedroom Apartment

My first apartment in NYC I found on Craigslist. My roommate was a Romanian guy who would occasionally pull back my curtain door and check if I was sleeping. Nice guy. Soon after that murder-waiting-to-happen living situation, my two friends in the city and I decided to move in together.

My two friends are women- Kat and Morgan. I was raised by women and always had a lot of girl friends so it felt natural. They're like my sisters. But, my entire life I'd been raised in a world where boy's and girl's rooms are separate. No scandalous co-ed business. But this is NYC and we're poor. Very, very poor.

We found a one bedroom apartment in Astoria, Queens that was perfect. It would've been *really* perfect for one of us. But we were poor. To afford an apartment in NYC you just have to keep adding people until the rent is low enough per person. It's a numbers game. Things that would seem ridiculous anywhere else seem normal in NYC if it means being able to make rent.

"No windows, the couch is on fire and there's a cobra in the bathroom? Sounds affordable, we'll take it."

We put all of our beds in the bedroom. It was like summer camp. More specifically, like a girl's summer camp and I was the creepy male counselor. Kat bought an actual bed and frame to sleep on. Morgan had a full-size air mattress that she would go on to use for two years. I claimed the twin-size mattress that the previous tenants left. It looked clean enough and was perfect because it was either that or sleep on the floor.

It sounds crazy but it worked. We were like a little family unit. All of us new to NYC, trying to figure out life. Figure out who we are. Survive. Eat pizza. Chase our dreams. Some nights we'd lie in bed chatting and laughing. Say our goodnights and try not to think about how we're all probably farting in our sleep.

One day Kat asked what we thought about one of her friends moving in with us. Three women + Paul in a one bedroom apartment?

SOLD.

That's my greatest fantasy come true: super cheap rent.

We held a family meeting, agreed and welcomed our new family member. "Three's Company" was now "Four's Company". We moved my bed out into the living room so the three women could share the bedroom.

People would always ask, "Paul, what do you all do for privacy?"

THAT'S EASY!

We don't.

The only privacy were the precious moments you had alone pooping or taking a shower. And thankfully our shower pressure was strong enough to cover up the sound of you crying. But we knew.

"Soap in your eyes again, huh?"

"What? Oh. Yeah. Soap."

Another frequent question was, "what happens if someone wants to bring someone home?"

EASY!

Celibacy.

All in all, I look back on those days as happy ones. We were a tight-knit bunch. I also think that living situation prepared me for marriage.

"Paul, take out the garbage."

"Paul, kill that bug."

"Paul, why are you crying?"

"Paul, why are you crying?"

"Paul, why are you crying?"

After daily cleaning out hair from the bathtub drain from three women, one woman doesn't seem too hard.

Haunting My In-laws

I've said it before and I'll say it again: I love my wife's parents. I genuinely look up to them and want to be like them when I get older. They're wise. Loving. Caring. Serve others and open their home to anyone who needs one.

They also only speak Korean in their house.

I do not speak Korean. I know like three words and play those on loop whenever I can shove them into conversation.

While my wife was on maternity leave, we lived with her parents in California for five weeks. Again, they ONLY speak Korean in their house.

I do not speak or understand Korean.

They DO speak English. (Not to me.) But they do.

So. For an entire month.

I.

Was.

Silent.

Just a quiet, white guy, silently observing a Korean family. I felt like a ghost haunting an older Korean couple. I'm pale, friendly-- I was Casper the Friendly Ghost. I'd watch, observe. Long to be part of the family. You know, ghost stuff.

When they wanted to speak to me directly, they would look and talk to my wife, who would then translate to me. So basically, my wife was a medium. I was Patrick Swayze, my wife was Whoopi Goldberg. But also Demi Moore.

"The ghost said he wants more kimchi, please."

DON'T CALL ME THE GHOST. Not helping.

Look. If they wanted to talk to me directly, with no translator. Be respectful. Use a Ouija board.

I love that they only speak Korean in their home. It's their home. There's something comforting about it. Home is your personal world safe from the outside world. Home is a place to be free and feel comfortable. Even though I couldn't understand anything, I still felt like I could understand everything. It's strange, but hometalk is all hometalk. Meals, family, church drama. There were even times when it would be just me and my mother-in-law in the kitchen and she'd have a full conversation with me in Korean before realizing she was talking to the white guy. Zero subtitles. We'd laugh. Then she'd say:

"You need to learn Korean."

"Neh."
("Yes"-- the most important word I know.)

That's my dream. To one day be fluent in Korean so I can speak freely with them. Meet them where they are. I want to show my respect and love for them by embracing their family's language. I love my wife so I love her family and her culture. I didn't even know what kimchi was before I met her, but now I eat bowls of it and know her mom makes the best. (True story: Esther's mom makes such delicious kimchi that it's made multiple grown men cry.) On the flip side, my wife embraces my family and culture too. I mean, before me, my wife had never eaten at Waffle House, gone to a college football game in Alabama or had flavorless, dry chicken for dinner. It's a beautiful thing to share your culture with loved ones.

Living with my in-laws for five weeks, hearing only Korean was extremely educational. Being immersed in another language is the best way to learn it. And after five weeks, I'm proud to say I learned two new words. Huge progress. By the time I'm 96 I'll be able to say a full sentence.

Honestly, not being able to speak for a month is very relaxing. Everyone around me has ZERO expectations of me contributing to conversations. Thank God. Didn't have to share opinions or ideas. I was just along for the ride. Arguments over where to eat for dinner? Hah!

Didn't matter, I was going to eat what was decided. My opinions on things happening in the news? Involuntary pass. It was the best. When you don't speak, no one can find out how dumb you actually are.

I was the agreeable, "Yes Man" all summer long. Because I had to be.

"Did you enjoy dinner?"

"Neh."

"Are you feeling well?"

"Neh."

"Can you take out the trash?"

"Neh."

We love this guy! At one point my mother-in-law did try to teach me the Korean alphabet. She found an extra children's workbook lying around. We made it two lessons.

"You need to practice."

"Neh."

She taught me how to write my name! That was exciting. I even remembered for about three hours how to write it before everything went out the window.

About week four Esther and I started feeling the itch to be in our own home again. No matter how comfortable you get in someone else's home, even if it's family, it's never *your* home. You don't have the same comforts or liberties to do as you please, like walking around naked or ordering Pizza Hut at midnight. While we craved our own space again, the hardest part of leaving was all the home cooked meals. So delicious. So healthy. Though, I'm not sure how many more weeks of seaweed soup or abalone porridge for breakfast I could stomach. Sometimes you just want a massive bagel loaded with cream cheese.

We left our time with her parents fuller, healthier and better parents. They took care of us while we took care of our baby boy. He got to soak up love from his grandparents and cousins. It was his first time being immersed in his Korean heritage. Constantly being spoken to in Korean. And just like his Appa, he still can't speak it.

Part II

My Month Before Marriage

This is the story of my final month being a bachelor. My final month of being a virgin. I held onto my v-card for 26 years before gifting it to my wife on our wedding night. AWESOME gift. VERY unused. Fresh. Clean. No previous owners.

We both waited till marriage to have sex. It's something we both believe in and we're glad we did it that way. Are we religious nuts? No. But are we religious? Yes. Nuts? Yes. I don't think I'm better than you if you have sex outside of marriage. Not that much at least. Decide what you want to do and stick to it. Sex isn't the core of marriage. That's not why I married my wife, to many dudes' disbelief. I'm in love with my wife and sex is just one of the many joys we share together. It'll be awkward and weird the first time. And I love that. I want to experience all the uncomfortableness, giggles and uncertainties present during the first time, *with her*. I don't want to be a seasoned pro going in, whipping out pre-practiced moves that other girls were into. I want to find out what my wife is into. Okay, that's the end of my TMI, over-sharing backstory.

One of my best friends suggested I document the days leading up to the wedding. He had to know what was going through my head. He had sex in high school so it's old news for him. But someone who kept a virtual chastity belt strapped on for two decades because of religious beliefs? WHAT'S HAPPENING IN THE HEAD OF THE GUY WHO'S A MONTH AWAY FROM HAVING SEX FOR THE FIRST TIME? Waiting so long for something that I wanted so badly, and it was finally about to happen. I had just moved into our new apartment that we would be living in. Just me in an empty apartment waiting for my bride. Prior to the new place I had always had roommates. In fact, my first couple years living in NYC I lived with all girls. Specifically, me and three girls in a one bedroom apartment. Then we moved and I shared a bedroom with one of the girls for a year. All platonic. Promise. God was watching the whole time. Living with those girls was like marriage boot camp. So, while I had never lived with a girlfriend before, I felt ready to handle myself in the terrain of living with my future wife.

Our wedding was on New Year's Eve. Each day leading up I wrote an entry. These are those entries.

Day 1:

FULLY MOVED. Assembled bed. Can't feel my back. My lower back particularly hurts very badly. Took forever to fall asleep because I'm alone in a new apartment– new sounds that are probably from ghosts of the tenants before me. Every shadow I'm certain is a demon. This new memory foam mattress swallows my lower back, not in a good way. Nyquil.

Day 2:

AM: It would feel strange waking up in a new apartment if this place didn't feel so right. Feeling like a king in this empty place. I'm the only one here and it's peaceful. I can go to the bathroom, leave the door open, walk to the kitchen and immediately go back to the bathroom (repeating this 4 times), without another person interrupting. Made coffee in the new coffee maker. Felt guilty about using the new coffee maker before fiance has moved in. Sat on a stool and drank my coffee. Just sat. Walked around apartment praying away evil demons for the safety of our home. Sincerely. I did that.

PM: Returned home after a show. Ate a frozen pizza from Duane Reade (the kind that tastes like greasy cardboard)((have to eat these before I'm not allowed to anymore)). Determined to build this damn TV stand. It has childlike directions and assembly requirements but still took me 2.5hrs to complete. No longer do I have a lower back. But I think I grew a chest hair. Fiancé is going to be devastated at how manly her future husband is. If the heating pipes in this new place don't stop whistling so loudly I'm going to peel every wood board from the floor and punch every square inch of the walls. Sleep.

Day 3:

AM: First Saturday waking up in the new place. The loneliness is almost a second person. We got a California King Size bed. I sleep on it like it's a single– on the edge like my body is a plank. Lower back is making a comeback. I'm already mapping out the creaky floor boards for when I come home late to my wife. Drank a whole pot of coffee. Not sharing an entire pot of coffee is what I imagine it feels like owning a coffee shop. This is how lonely, rich guys live.

PM: Home late. 7,642 packages for us in the lobby (actually 5) that I have to carry up by myself. My existence is opening boxes then breaking them down. There are boxes that come inside of other boxes like an Amazon Prime Russian Doll. I don't remember a life in which I wasn't constantly opening, unpacking, breaking down, folding, carrying cardboard boxes. Ran into the super in the elevator and asked how he was doing and his response was, "long day, so tired from moving all the stacks of cardboard boxes, going to have some wine." LOUD AND CLEAR MAN I'M SORRY.

Contemplating just keeping the remaining cardboard boxes in the apartment and taking them out one a day over the course of a week because I feel guilty. The whistling from the radiator is inviting me to buy an ax. Need to conquer the radiator before fiance moves in.

Day 4:

AM: THE RADIATOR WHISTLING IS ALL-CONSUMING. I am the whistling and it is me. It's like I'm a dog and my apartment is constantly blowing a dog whistle. Thinking of giving a name to the radiator whistle because it's starting to shape who I am as a person. It's not long before I start whistling back. Walked around in the buff after my shower. Wow. I've been missing out. Another whole pot of coffee before church.

PM: First dinner at the apartment with the fiance. I don't want her to leave. This is our place. She makes it feel like home. I don't want to go back to spending evenings alone with the whistling radiator. Fiance took me grocery shopping because she knows I was planning to live off granola bars and ramen noodles before she moves in. Can't wait for her to move in. I don't use the TV or anything in the apt, I literally just sit alone in silence. Like I'm just waiting for my mom to pick me up from school. If I drop something or make a loud noise I immediately envision my neighbors rushing over to yell at me. I used my power drill at midnight. I assume I'm now their mortal enemy. // Home late after a show and was welcomed home by the warm SATAN RADIATOR. Need to pray around the house more.

Day 5:

AM: The key to taking out more cardboard boxes is to rip off the address label. That way the super doesn't see the name of who left a forest-worth of boxes in the garbage area. I left the stickers on. I'm a coward. Even if I took them off I know he'd know it was me. He can smell the guilt. We walked by each other the other morning and he didn't even make eye contact with me. Thinking about taping some Dove chocolates to the stack of boxes for him (they're delicious and have an inspirational message inside). Woke up late today. Funny how the whistling radiator keeps me up at night but can't wake me up in the morning. Selfish. We live in a fallen world. Waiting to ask the super to fix the radiator. Can't let him see that I have more cardboard boxes waiting for him in the apartment. Was in a rush and didn't get to eat any of the groceries fiance bought me.

PM: Oh look MORE BOXES WAITING FOR ME IN THE LOBBY. Grabbed my stack. Opened them all. There was a t-shirt in one of the packages that said in sparkles "Daddy's Other Girl". I'm 95% sure that was not on our registry. Asked fiance about it when she came over. We discovered that I grabbed another tenants package on accident. Oh no. No. No. I'm fast becoming the Newman of the apartment building. I committed a federal offense. Fiance walked me to the neighbor's apt to return it like I'm some kid who broke a window playing baseball. He was gracious. For dinner I wanted pizza but instead fiance cooked me a delicious, healthy meal. Something about men dying sooner than women. Assembled a bathroom rack and set up the TV as a team. Start feeling lonely as we complete the tasks because I know that means she leaves soon. She packed a lunch for me for tomorrow. Back to being a man in his cave. Gave the bird to the radiator before bed.

Day 6:

AM: Woke up super early for the gym. I've heard abs and muscles do NOT piss off fiances. I take out more cardboard boxes as I leave in the cover of the early morn. It's 30 blocks to the gym and I forgot my Metro card but have my credit card for some reason. Took a cab to the gym. Hate myself the whole ride. Couldn't stop shaking my head. Future dad Paul is furious. I'm not a zillionaire. Felt guilty about the $8 cab fare so I walk the 30 blocks home after my workout. Worth it. Every time I leave the apartment in the morning I pray I don't run into the super. I ran into the super. Like a monster, I tell him about the whistling radiator. I say "sorry" five times and "thank you" three times in the duration of our 30-second convo. I'm thinking a Dunkin Donuts gift card for Christmas gift. Had a PB&J for breakfast because I'm 12.

PM: Came home and went number two. Feels pharaoh-like knowing there won't be anyone else already in the bathroom. // Home late after doing comedy. Eat more groceries. Two bags-worth of groceries in Manhattan cost $257,894. Phone call with fiance. Having her on speaker phone makes it feel like she's here. Her voice fills the room and comforts me. The creaky floor boards are a good warning if an intruder breaks in to kill us. Hopefully the whistling has a disorienting effect on bad guys, like a flash-bang grenade so that fiance and I can escape. Our barricade of cardboard boxes helps. Pray for us.

Day 7:

AM: Super knocks on the door. I know it's him because I hear the janitor-of-a-stadium-amount of keys jingling as he walks up. This is it. He's finally going to fix the whistling radiator. This is the day I am liberated and live in peace. He interrupted my morning devotionals but I know God will understand. I explain the whistling situation, apologizing 8,492 times. He smiles and shrugs and says, "they all do that." OH THANK GOD SO THE WHOLE APT BUILDING IS FULL OF PEOPLE ON THE VERGE OF MURDER. I ask him about replacing the shiny thing. Borderline panic in my voice. "Nah, it's fine. Let me know if you see leaking." I say thank you 98 times. On his way out he asks if I have anymore furniture coming. I see the dread in his eyes as he asks. I say we have a large couch coming. He nods and smiles with his mouth closed. We're getting him a nice bottle of wine for Christmas. Install a towel rack on the back of bathroom door. The kind that you suction on like it's a toy. In my head I am Tim The Tool Man Taylor. Fiance texts that I should let my hair grow so "we" can decide a style. "What's yours is mine and mine is yours" applies to hair. Thankfully I no longer have the responsibility of styling my hair.

PM: "EEEEEEEEEEEEEEEEEEEEEE". Hello dearest whistling. My precious. My sweet. How thoughtful of you to pierce my ears and soul before I even take off my shoes. Unwrapped two more packages. Packages every day, forever and always. UPS feels like a desperate ex-lover trying to win me back who just won't get the hint. No matter how many trampled boxes I throw out, there are fresh ones waiting for me when I come home. As a kid I loved opening boxes. Now it's like when a parent catches their kid smoking and makes them smoke a whole pack. But I feel like smoking. Remind myself to be thankful for the gifts in the box. I'm such a child. Fearing a nightmare where a box opens me like a box. It'll use one of its kitchen knives because he doesn't have scissors yet even though he could just buy a pair instead of ruining the food knife they got as a wedding gift. The hallway smells like weed smoke every night. Now I know it's from someone coping with their whistling radiator. I still have not unpacked any of my belongings. Living out of a suitcase. Feels like I'm only a visitor here until fiance moves in. Plus my stuff will be rearranged when she moves in her stuff. I type all of this in my boxers because I am my only roommate. I'm days away from being house robe guy.

Day 8:

AM: Bed is too comfortable to leave for gym. Thank God I don't notice the whistling this morning. Drowned out by THE CONSTRUCTION OUTSIDE MY WINDOW. Maybe the radiator knows how I feel now. Mashed an avocado on bread for breakfast. No toaster yet. Baggies of carrots, apple slices for lunch because I'm a rabbit.

PM: Fiance orders me food to be delivered when I get home after a late show. I wouldn't even do that for me. She knows how to love me better than I know how to love me. Pizza and wings. Was literally on the verge of tears reading the text. TWO MORE HUGE BOXES. Fun and easy shoving them up the stairs down the hallway like some sort of box relay. Feeling spooked tonight. Hear a buzzing/ scratching noise near the front door. Stared at door for 2 minutes. Nothing. Whistling drowned it out. Walked by the electronic trash can and the lid opened. Jumped back against the wall like a housewife from a soap opera. Eating all the pizza and wings to console me. She did this to make me go to the gym tomorrow.

Day 9:

AM: Offensively early gym session. Waited 20 min for bus in 30 degrees. Only wearing a hoodie. Fiance would never let me be so stupid. It's her bachelorette party this weekend. Wish I could chaperone. Eat leftover pizza for breakfast and lunch. Fiance texts that there's a surprise waiting for me at the apt when I get home tonight. I hope it's food.

PM: Actually laugh out loud seeing 3 big boxes waiting in the apt lobby. Stack them and push them on the floor to my door like a football player shoving a sled as punishment for missing a tackle. First thing I see when I walk in is our new coffee table. Fiance and her sis put it together. With tools and everything. Even took the cardboard box outside. Fist pump with pride. Feels like she built an entire house. I love her so much. A neatly wrapped gift in gold paper is on said coffee table. Is it mine? Should I open it? Is this the "surprise" waiting for me or is the surprise that she assembled the coffee table? I check the kitchen for "surprise" baked goods like I'm ransacking the apt. Each non-cookie-filled cupboard I grow a little more frantic. Text fiance about the gold gift. Radiator is whistling for me to open it. Can't find out if it's for me because psycho bachelorette party rules won't allow her to communicate with me all weekend. The gold wrapped gift has become my apple in the Garden of Eden. Either way, I can't open it. There's no way I could re-wrap it well enough to make it seem unopened. The curiosity is KILLING me. Wish I could turn up the whistling to drown out my curiosity. The two bills left directly next to the gift are definitely for me.

Day 10:

AM: This Cali King Size memory foam bed hates the gym. Doesn't want me to be shredded for my betrothed. Across town to pick up another table for the apt. Our home is now 86% tables. All sizes and assortments. 4 chairs but 17 tables. Breakfast is a Red Bull and cookie because fiance isn't here to reprimand me. THREE MORE BOXES FOR THE LOVE OF ALL THAT IS HOLY. Record a podcast episode with a comedian pal. He says he only noticed the whistling after I mentioned it and it's all he hears now. I'm not crazy.

PM: Late night comedy show in the Bronx then friend's bachelor party. Arrive home about an hour before I'm usually waking up. Fiance would never allow this because she knows I hate it. Can't wait to be married and pull the "wife needs me home" card. BFF stays the night. A final bro-over while the place is still a bachelor pad. He also only hears the whistling. We eat pizza and candy. Feels good to be in middle school.

Day 11:

AM: So tired that I feel hungover. Shower then church. // Home from church less than 2 minutes. THREE MORE BOXES. ON THE LORD'S DAY?! My neighbors hear me laugh and huff as I carry the trinity of boxes down the hall. Boxes come in threes. Always. Numbers have significance in the Bible for stuff like plagues and doom. "And then the Lord sent a multitude of waves of 3 boxes by 3 boxes upon the whistling apartment." Assemble a kitchen rack. Tear down more boxes. I am now a full-time warehouse employee. Going to ask for a box cutter and a pair of Dickie's for Christmas.

PM: Have dinner with fiance. She was only gone for a weekend but it felt like a month. Two hours at dinner with her makes me feel more at home than 72 hours alone in our new apartment. Another late show tonight. Considering sleeping on the carpet next to the radiator to ensure I wake up for the gym tomorrow.

Day 12:

AM: Dizzy from sleepiness. No gym. Counsel myself mentally for why getting fit isn't what the wedding is about. Fiance has already agreed to marry me. No take backs. Justify staying in bed. When I'm married leaving will be impossible. Treat myself by only breaking down two boxes, save the rest for night Paul (sucker). Text fiance good morning. She doesn't ask about the gym.

PM: Wedding planning with fiance. She asks what all has been delivered to the apt. Lots of brown cardboard boxes. Empty, soulless boxes. Were I homeless this would be my heaven. Everything that we get looks the same– pots, plates, racks, utensils. I genuinely don't know what we have and I'm the one who takes it all out. Open, put away, break down, repeat. I use one plate, one cup, sometimes a fork. All else is gray matter. // Only one light box in the lobby. "And so God saw Paul's weary shoulders and granted him ease." There's no one around to hug. In the box is a wood board thing. My mind races thinking of all the exciting things we'll do with this wood board thingy. I don't read its label. Better off not knowing. Hate morning Paul for leaving the remaining stack of boxes. Lay on our carpet and listen to sermon. Maybe words of God will smite this ear-piercing radiator. Halfway through I worry about the potential of neighbors hearing a pastor through loudspeakers while trying to be intimate. Fiance texts me to go to bed early for the gym.

Day 13:

AM: I did it. I'm out of bed for the gym. 5:30AM. Under the blanket of twilight I take a secret load of boxes out (the super still knows it's me). I make a run for the bus as it's pulling up. I forgot my bus pass. Walk back home shouting "of course" out loud to myself like a disappointed coach. Wait 20 min for another bus. Repeat "fiances love abs" in my head. Keg-stand a pot of coffee when I get back. Need more caffeine. Do my morning devotions sans clothes a la Garden of Eden.

PM: Fiance waiting for me at apt. She set up our new couch and took out a bunch of boxes because she reads how much I complain about them on here. I'm marrying a superhero of a woman. A saint. She cares for me far more than I deserve. I am a child. The box the couch came in waits for me to take out. It's the size of a city bus. Maybe we can rent it out as an apt within our apt. I black out and order 6,000 tacos and guacamole as my contribution for the night. More wedding planning and a little bit of the movie "Love Actually". Gross. Thankful for our actual love. No amount of Hugh Grant's awkward British flirting drowns out the sound of whistling. Want to fast forward life like a movie to the part where fiance is wife and doesn't have to leave me in this apt alone. Will try to be fully clothed when sitting on the couch before she moves in but I just. don't. know.

Day 14:

AM: UGGGGHHHHHH. Fiance-motivated gym session to get offensively shredded for our wedding. I go early because I like being up before the sun. Makes me feel more productive than the sun. Post-shower Paul wants to sit on that fresh, new sofa. Just once. Really quick. I put on boxers then sit. No thrill being a prude. Catch myself falling asleep as I drink coffee. Tried to sit and read some Word of the Lord but just stared at Lucifer's whistling radiator for 23 minutes. Maybe radiator is Satan incarnate and is trying to drive me out of this soon-to-be love-filled married home. Going to draw crosses on it.

PM: Fiance's birthday dinner even though her birthday is tomorrow. I've never heard of "responsibly scheduling stuff." Might as well be quantum physics (or really anything that has numbers in it). I booked a show on her actual birthday. Classic Disney villain move. She was incredibly gracious. Waaaaay cooler than I would've been. As the youngest child I've had some tantrums. I take her to sushi. To the same place she took me for a birthday long ago where I realized for the first time I wanted to date her. I bring her a dozen pink roses and a card. I stress that this is not all I got her. The card is a "Wife Birthday" card but I scratched out "wife" and wrote "fiance". She's so much better at gift-giving than me. Thank God I'm marrying her so I can learn from her. My face is the heart-eye emoji the whole dinner. HEAVEN'S TO BETSY I'M MARRYING A BABE. We feel like a rom-com sometimes. In all the mushiest, gooiest, disgusting, up-and-down, serendipitous and heart-warming ways imaginable. The more that makes you gag and your eyes roll the better. // Home solo. Only one small box. Thank you merciful Creator of the Universe. Fancy vases. Never thought I'd be a fancy vase owner one day. Maybe next I'll get an eye monocle and horse-drawn carriage. Listening to Mariah Carey's "All I Want for Christmas" infinity times because that's the only Christmas song.

Day 15:

AM: Angel and Devil argue on shoulders: stay in bed or go to gym. Angel wins. I lose. Gym to work on those abs fiance has reminded me all about. // Turn on Christmas music. Internet keeps dropping. Mariah Carey sounds like she's driving through a tunnel. Every time I click refresh the wifi cuts out. Then back in. This post took 16 hours to write. The wifi signal knows I'm watching it. Any time I glance away it disconnects. A perk of paying for Internet is not having Internet. It's in cahoots with the radiator. Or maybe radiator whistling cuts the wifi connection? Hoax? Conspiracy? Today is my sweet fiance's birthday. Thank God I bought her flowers yesterday.

PM: Like any good, loving, dutiful, selfless fiance, I do a comedy show tonight. Really racking up brownie points by not seeing her on her birthday. I brag about her to anyone who will listen at show. Bitterly cold out. So cold I have two holes in my shirt from nipples poking through. Two small boxes greet me in the lobby. I am their father and they my cardboard children. I run a cardboard box orphanage. I am Father Cardboard. A serving dish and glass vase thingy. Both I'd probably use as plate and cup in my earlier bachelor years. I'm an adult. We bought a couch. A couch really makes a home and holds memories. Sucks even having thoughts while in the apt alone. Fiance isn't here to share with, make jokes, annoy. Big city buses pick up and drop off right outside my window. Once you get past the screeching brakes, grumpy engine, honking and lunatics yelling, it's quite soothing. Fiance and I will joke about these things together one day soon.

Day 16:

AM: Friday. Every day feels like Monday but today is "Friday". It's negative 1.86 trillion degrees outside. No way I'm ever leaving this Hot Pocket sleeve of warmth in bed. I envision Paul with belly and pale man boobs and go to the gym. After I buy two cases of beer for fiance's bday gathering at apt with friends later. I joke with cashier that I feel like an alcoholic buying two cases at 8am. She asks for ID. I walk by the super gathering cardboard and trash. I say 'good morning' too loudly like that will distract him from seeing my name on all the package labels.

PM: It's as cold as Superman's lair. As a Florida boy anything colder than 50 feels like Jack hanging off the door in the water. Late to fiance's bday gathering because of a show. Final show doing all my virgin material. Thank God. Already writing married guy stuff that fellow humans can relate to. Text fiance I'm on my way home. No response. Killing it in the prioritize-her-bday department. (she was preparing a plate of wings for me). Two boxes waiting for me in the lobby. I adopt them on the spot. Glad fiance & co. are there to witness my box struggle. Her friends always make me feel like I'm a friend too. No whistling in the apt. Freezing cold in the apt. Touche radiator....touche. Heat broken for the night. We can hear our teeth chatter in peace. Careful what you wish for. I drink 3.6 beers with the girls and already feel post-Vegas hungover. Coconut water. Cold leftover wings. 14 sleeves of cookies. Finally give fiance her big bday gift. She understands that it's also her Christmas. One day when I have money she will be showered with more gifts. We put the new duvet (had to look up this spelling) cover on the bed for me to test drive before marriage. Wow. No idea sheets were allowed to feel this soft. I come from a life of sandpaper blankets and old comforters roommates were throwing out. Feel guilty sleeping all night because I'm using it without fiance. Feels like a cloud, so that helps with the guilt.

Day 17:

AM: Good morning, headache. Feel like I just respawned after an EDM festival. 3.6 beers did this to me. My future kids will bully me. Coach Paul yells at Paul Paul for consuming alcohol. It's snowing. Agreed to help fiance and friend move stuff. So blessed to do it with a headache in the snow. Radiator is laughing up a storm. I find a bag of scones in the kitchen and immediately eat two. Text fiance to ask if bag of scones was for me. Thank God. Dishes piled in the sink. I almost do them. Almost. Leave them for PM Paul. Man he's a sucker.

PM: Do an afternoon comedy show for kids. They love the poop stuff. Me too. Gig last night was final night of doing virgin jokes. Buh-bye. Help at holiday party then do gift exchange with fiance. She won. Come home and pack my suitcase. Fiance texts me packing list. I would've packed one jeans, 1.5 shirts and maybe a toothbrush if not for her. We give our super a nice bottle of wine, chocolates and card. Should've given it to him in a cardboard box with a wink and elbow jab. AM Paul left me dishes so I do them to be the bigger man. Eat cookies as a prize. LEAVE ME ALONE WEDDING DIET. Tomorrow I fly to Florida to spend one final Xmas with momma as Unmarried Paul. Our last mom-son Christmas hoorah. Tomorrow I leave this apt Engaged Paul. When I return I will be Husband Paul. Married to the most life-changingly beautiful woman ever. My person. AND THEN her and I can conquer this whistling radiator together. Forever. Like Romeo & Juliet without the dying and annoying way people speak. BTW- I'll be continuing this while in Florida at mom's house where there is no whistling radiator. Here's a pic of the demon:

Day 18:

AM: Up at 4:15AM. Set 179 alarms so I don't miss my flight. Barely cognizant of my existence. So tired. Heartfelt goodbye to radiator. Mixed emotions like you'd have saying farewell to a childhood bully to whom you've grown accustomed. Check cost of Uber fare and decide $1.2mil is out of my range. Wait for an airport bus in Harlem at 5AM. Thirty years later I arrive to airport. I want Dunkin' Donuts so bad. A hologram of fiance is barring me from standing in line to buy a strawberry frosted & sprinkles donut. I buy regret-flavored Greek yogurt. Pass out on plane.

PM: Bff/groomsman picks me up. So good to be met by the humid warmth of Florida. It's like a sticky hug and I love it. Surprise mom and grammy at church. // Momma's home I get to choose between three different bedrooms to sleep in. A king's crown and scepter grow out of my body. Compared to my apt this is Buckingham Palace. This would cost $9trillion/mo in the city. Keeping with tradition we pick up a baby Xmas tree from a bearded man. Mom makes me grilled cheese for dinner. Finish with a bowl of cereal. I'm either the saddest bachelor or the happiest kid. All I hear is peace and quiet here. I should record this silence and play it in my radiator's face to show how it's done. Sad fiance is not here with me. After the wedding never again will I come home to Florida without her. Choose older brother's old room to sleep in tonight and there's nothing he can do about it.

Day 19:

AM: Opie jumps on my bed and wakes me up by licking my face. We are a living Norman Rockwell painting. A boy and his lazy-eyed dog. Notice lump on Opie's chin. Coming here for a week after living in NYC is like being an astronaut in quarantine readjusting to earth. Drive mom to work. Oh how the tables have turned.

PM: Vet says Opie has bone cancer in his jaw. "Best bet is to spoil him these last 6-8 months." His whole life is treats, walks and naps so not sure how to spoil him more. Today sucks. Mom and I cry in the parking lot. Wish fiance could teleport here. Opie oblivious that he has cancer on his face. This is the dog I picked out from the litter of babies from our old dog. My pal. Mom's furry comforter. Tonight I scratch his back a little more, let him lick my face a little more. One day me and wife will have to explain this kind of stuff to our children.

Day 20:

AM: Why am I waking up before 9AM? Body clock is a traitor. Has no place in my body. I'm home for Xmas. I should wake up only when I have to leave Florida completely. Bears hibernate and that's their vacation. There are no honking horns and crazy people yelling outside my windows like in city. Only birds chirping and moms making breakfast in the kitchen. Mom gives Opie some food treats. Mom and I go to local coffee shop. Normally I like to stay home and have zero human interaction. Local bakeries will pry a man from home. The fun part of running into people is receiving praise for getting married. Some praise throws me off. All I did was get lucky enough to have a woman contractually agree to never leave me. Simple stuff. I'm like a dog wagging his tail with his tongue out whenever someone asks about fiance. Still haven't decorated our little Charlie Brown Christmas tree. Mom and I will probably wait till Dec 26th. Busy with things like deciding our mother-son dance for the wedding.

PM: Cracker Barrel for dinner with mom and grammy. Very diverse. 99% white people and 1% probably white. Our entire bill is two pennies. This dinner would cost twelve mortgages in the city. Should have eaten more free biscuits. // Home late after good catch up with friend/groomsman. Thought about not telling fiance we ate Krystal's burgers. Nostalgia is the real attacker of wedding diet. If I'm just Richard Simmons-in-shape and not Zac Effron-in-shape she. will. still. marry. me. I'm safe…ish. Probably.Knowing fiance will accept me for whatever shape I am only makes me want to get borderline sinfully ripped. No matter what age, coming home late feels like sneaky high school coming in late. Won't be able to tip-toe home late at new apt because wood floorboards creak like an aging pirate ship when you so much as glance at them. Wishing I was with fiance to help with wedding stuff. Loving someone brings with it missing them and constantly pushing out thoughts of 'Final Destination' tragedies following them throughout the day. Go to bed listening to Opie have weird dreams. Me too buddy, me too.

Day 21:

AM: Herculean effort to get out of bed. Opie licks my face post licking his butt. Angel mother greets me with sausage biscuits and coffee. Leaving bed was a good choice. 4 hour time difference with fiance. I don't text her good morning. Don't want to risk waking her from her princess slumber. Choosing to text and disturb or neglect to text is Sophie's choice. She texts me.

PM: Mom and I get our ears candled. Lady shoves a wax cone in your ear and lights it on fire. Think witchcraft but on a massage table. It clears your ears out. We joke about being able to 'think clearer' now. Seinfeld level stuff. Mom-son dates used to be slushies or pie. We eat Arby's for lunch to be nostalgic. "I'm not being unhealthy I'm being nostalgic" is my new defense. War against wedding diet is in full force. I make up for it by looking at an apple and eating single bites of cookies (ate the whole thing) at home. These days are the calm before the storm. Not a bad storm. More like a hurricane of love storm. Fiance texts me picture of her in wedding makeup. Didn't realize I was MARRYING A MOVIE

STAR. She'll be saying "I do" to a guy who looks like he shaved blindfolded while getting a $12 haircut. We put lights on our little Xmas tree. Mom makes the same meal Esther made me my first night in new apt. Won't say whose was better until after I'm under signed legal marriage contract with fiance. Going to bed trying to guilt Morning Paul to wake up early to exercise. Guilt is a great alarm clock.

Day 22:

AM: Please dear God let it be the wedding already. The anticipation is more stressful than the planning. Up early. Solo drive to the river to watch the sunrise and do pull-ups. Idk if men tear up looking at a sunrise but Paul does. At least I got buff to compensate. Devotions by the Christmas tree. Stare at birds outside for 7 minutes. I make a wicked cool grandpa and a lame 26 y.o.

PM: Realize I've been so relaxed because I haven't had to tear down any boxes in 4 days. Sample more cookies because they're lonely on that plate. Lunch with friend. Restaurant owner tells me my face is thin and motions with hand that my cheeks are gaunt. THANKS TRYING TO FIX THAT AT YOUR RESTAURANT. He doesn't know I need -.00002% body fat for hot irresistible-to-wife wedding bod. Mentally on verge of exploding because I haven't been on stage in 4 days. Can only force new jokes into conversation with others so much. Mom and I eat dinner with friends. Fiance is in CA slaving away at wedding stuff. I do my part by whining about one reception song. Real smooth. Make a big deal about one song. So helpful to our ceremony of SELFLESS LOVE PAUL. Maybe I can have my own bottle and bib one day. Watch "A Christmas Story" with momma. Opie sits betwixt. He farts often. Not sure if it's new food farts, medicine farts or cancer farts. Opie sleeping in big bed with me tonight. Farts and all. This is the last person (living thing) to share a bed with me until my wife. Will have to relearn cuddling with someone that isn't furry.

Day 23:

AM: Swedish pancakes. All of them. No siblings around to share. All. For. Me. Fiance and I will make Swedish pancakes for our kids one day. Probably organic-gluten-free-range-whole-oat-granola version since they'll be fancy city kids. Get a haircut. Ask for "itsy bitsy tiny slight clean-up on the sides and neck." She gives me the 2007 Britney Spears break-down look. Momma assures me it looks fine. Benefit of such a beautiful fiance is it doesn't really matter how I look at the ceremony.

PM: Lunch with friend at local diner. Food is so cheap I think we now legally own part of the restaurant. Don't order the french fries because fiance has spies watching. She's doing a ton more wedding prep today. Guilt of not being there to help makes me want to eat french fries. Got a package at mom's house. THEY FOUND ME. // Dinner with Grammy. She reminds me my hair is darker. Less blonde now. Almost brown. I will now think only thoughts about my hair being not blonde for the rest of life. When she asks if I "work on

TV" it feels like she's roasting me. She genuinely doesn't know, but I still say "touche" in my head. I perform in front of TVs in bars regularly. Catch up with friends at local brewery. Drink water to feel like a chaperone. I'm two Christmases away from asking for fanny pack. When people tell me how cheap rent is here all of a sudden all I can see is that spinning tunnel scene from "Charlie and the Chocolate Factory". Opie sleeps in bed with me again tonight. Just two bachelor dudes curled up in a ball holding it together until morning.

Day 24:

AM: Mom and I put on body armor, inject caffeine, say prayers and go to Walmart. Last minute frenzy for stuff we'll all forget in a week. Jesus' head is exploding. People getting cartfuls of Steven Seagal movies and wouldn't-even-feed-that-to-my-dog candy from the 800% OFF bins. As I wait for mom I chat with a blue vest employee. This is my only performance in a week. Bombing hard. Finally get a huge laugh when I say "moms, they just grow up so fast". It's the funniest thing this woman has heard. I know my demo. "Clean up on aisle 3, Paul's killing." We survive Walmart. Mom makes me more coffee because I'm being a baby.

PM: Phone call with fiance. Hard to take heed the advice "enjoy each moment before the wedding." I want all those moments to be with fiance. Do push-ups and brag to fiance for praise and affirmation. Before wedding maybe I can ask bridesmaids makeup person to airbrush on movie star abs. // Christmas Eve church service. I pick up Grammy. Reminds me of my used-to-be-so-much-blonder hair. She's on Comedy

Central Roast Battle this Spring. After service we come home for Swedish meatballs. Family tradition. I clean the dishes. Only took me 26 years to finally gift that to my mom. I put Opie's present under the tree– a toy slice of pizza. Stuff goodies in mom's stocking. Not putting out cookies and milk for Santa. Mom and I are too tired to wake up and eat them in the middle of the night.

Day 25:

AM: Awake to throbbing headache. Merry Christmas. I'm the only person who gets hungover from water. Opie bites his toy pizza slice present once then walks away. Good emotional prep for kids one day. Mom and I agree to look at our stockings later when we're awake. We are Santa for each other. I fill her stocking when I think she's asleep. She does the same. Neither of us are actually asleep. Just waiting till we hear the other clear from stocking area. We make breakfast for the family and take 17,000 photos in front of Xmas tree. I love adult Christmas. It's all gift cards for coffee.

PM: Nap after taking nap. Opie actively avoids his pizza chew toy. He has cancer he can do whatever he wants. Life is a blur of eating sweet treats. Wedding body is fading like Marty McFly's photo in 'Back to the Future'. Mom and I exchange stockings. She gives me a throwback gift I always asked for as a kid. Cheese Wiz and crackers. I have the diet and wishes of a hobo. I give her gift certificate for mani/pedi. Hibernation nap. Talk with fiance. Extra gooey lovey Christmas words. To everyone else we sound like babies cooing and giggling at each other. She really is the best gift I've ever received. // Evening meal at Aunt and Uncle's. Eat as if I'm about to be dropped off on a deserted island. Home for a silly movie. Brains turned off. Simple Christmas. Jesus loves you. Opie and I go to sleep in a cloud of each other's post-Xmas farts. Each time he farts he looks at his butt then walks away. He is gassing me to sleep.

Day 26:

AM: That type of wake up where you forget where you are. Take an entire CVS worth of vitamin C. Promise myself to be productive today. Productive for first 5 minutes following a cup of coffee. Sit with Opie. Just sit. Must eat healthy today must eat healthy today. Eat some Cheese Wiz and crackers. Fiance deploys wedding prep list action plan for the day. I send a whole email and look at an excel sheet. I'm a big boy.

PM: Visit with friends. Get a marriage devotional book. Waiting for someone to give me a magical sword and riddle for this journey for which I am about to embark. Friend's marriage advice– "she's always right." Scary thing is fiance actually is always right. I will have to fake being frustrated about wife's wise counsel to fit in with future husband pals (will ask fiance if this is good decision). This is the woman who informed me that washing my face before bed every night was a thing. Every night. Genuinely thought only girls do that. Dinner with mom and Grammy. Last supper with them as non-married Paul. More wedding action phone calls with fiance. Huge perk of wedding is there will only be one. Mom and I watch Goosebumps before bed. Double-down on being a child one final night. Glass of chocolate milk for night cap. Check in for our flights. Frontier. God help us. Sell the house, life insurance policy and 18 quarts of blood to pay for baggage and seating fees. None of it matters. Tomorrow I see my betrothed. Excited for a week of kimchi and putting on permanent rings.

Day 27:

AM: HEADACHE. FOR FREE. FREE HEADACHE. HAVE ALL OF THEM. HEADACHE IS GOOD ALARM CLOCK. Wait around all day for flight tonight. My suitcase has been packed for two days. Opie is increasingly suspicious of bag commotion in the house. Feed him treats. Drop him off at kennel and feel like negligent father. Last day in Florida with momma. Instead of being useful human being I eat snacks on couch. Prescribe myself Cheese Wiz each time stress and nerves creep into head.

PM: Fully engaged with frontal headache before traveling. So blessed. Aunt, Uncle and cousins pick up me and momma for airport. My suitcase almost doesn't fit. Bags stack floor to ceiling in car. Can't budge. Foreshadow of flight. Headache massages frontal lobe. Mom has TSA pre-check and skips through security. I go in peasant line. It's like Black Friday shopping but just the waiting in lines part (pre-cyber sale days). We are cows being herded without sweet relief of slaughter. Make it to our gate. A nursery of screaming children is stationed in our area. Satan doesn't want us going to San Diego. Past Paul hates Future Paul and booked Frontier. Present Paul always suffers. No cover on our armrest. Just metal bar. Frontier is public transit of the sky. We are the people who would've drowned on the Titanic. Peasants. Immediately start eating bag of snack rations mom packed. 5 1/2 hr flight. No music. No movie. No reading. Can't sleep. Just sit and stare straight ahead for 2 hours like serial killer. Man next to me has loud music playing from earbuds. For 3 hours I fantasize about confronting him/ killing him/ asking to stop/ opening cabin door/ combination of all four. We land. Mom's head about to explode like in Total Recall. Arrive to hotel just before 2AM. Tell hotel clerk I'm checking in for my wedding. He says "congrats… is this your first marriage?" I burn down the hotel. Let him know he should give me room key and just stop. Finally here in San Diego. Going to be VERY married VERY soon.

Day 28:

AM: Body pulls prank on me with time change. Wake at 6AM. Classic schtick. Finally see fiance. We embrace in hotel lobby. Audience of half-asleep tourists eating french toast drink in our love. Feels like a month has passed. All stress and tiredness dissolves as we hug. Fiance's father takes us– mom, brother & wife on San Diego tour. If you hate perfect weather and beautiful cities don't move here.

PM: Mom, brother & wife, one groomsman meet fiance's family for first time. NAIL IT. As if we rehearsed together for months. The two older brothers talk older brother stuff like beer. I chime in with jokes and bomb. Having two older brothers is too much pressure. Fiance's mom comments on my shrunken in cheeks. Fiance now feels responsible to feed me. How did I win this? Eat the most delicious homemade Korean meal I've ever had. My family eats like we just got out of prison. Lots of hugs and thank you's. When there are language barriers just keep saying thank you and laugh occasionally. Help fiance with wedding prep. She's unstoppable. All are exhausted. Sleep.

Day 29:

AM: alksjglkhsalkdgjlskhglka. Hot mama gimme that headache! Love the sinus pressure that's taken residence in my brain. Perfect for wedding preparations. Just waking up makes me feel hungover. Got wasted on "sleep" and "awakening". Eat imitation breakfast in hotel lobby. Fiance and I pick up our MARRIAGE LICENSE. We are officially halfway married. Begin decorating church gym for reception. Use scissor lift to hang 100,000 miles of string lights from rafters. We are no longer bridal party. We are factory workers. Wedding prep is fun way to realize true calling as blue collar warehouse employee. What is a lower back? Inhale table of kimchi and kalbi beef for lunch.

PM: Hang lights and repeat. Cut flowers. Spray paint flowers (murder?). Hang lights more and more and forever hanging lights always hanging lights. Sushi family dinner. We order two boats of sushi. Waitress tells me her daughter floats on them sometime. Continue to eat off boat where her daughter sometimes sits. Back to warehouse job hanging lights for wedding. Slower this time from overeating sushi. Drink half a beer. Slow body. Belly grows larger. Too late to elope? Just kidding. Eloping is too easy and stress-free. Put fun lanterns on string lights. Late night pick up from the airport. Taxi driver Paul feels like Tired Paul. Return to momma's hotel room where it's peaceful. Calm of momma's home follows where ever she goes. Say prayers and thank God for incredibly devoted, helpful friends and family. Don't deserve them. They have no idea how much they have to help tomorrow. We will all be factory workers.

Day 30:

AM: Body feels like I slept underneath bag of bricks. Sit up in bed. Immediately stress eat muffin. Stare at self in mirror for 10 min just staring. Who is that guy? This is day before wedding. All the final thoughts are flooding. Eat more muffin. Older brother goes into older brother mode and acts as caretaker of my day. Set up tables at church. Set up decoration things. All is a blur. Seconds slip by faster. So real so real so real so real.

PM: Rehearsal. For my wedding. We are having wedding rehearsal for my wedding where I will marry my dream woman best friend. Fiance is stuck with me forever and ever amen. Thank God. We are all smelly and tired from setting up. But we are in the chapel. We are practicing being husband and wife instead of just fiancé and fiancé. So many hugs happening. Rehearsal dinner. Fiance looks stunning. Family and friends gather. Older brother gives best man speech and we are all crying. I can't make eye contact when he makes eye contact. Tears. Laughter. Love-filled deep-hearted tears. So much said even in pauses of silence. More speeches more tears and laughter. Running out of tissues. Don't deserve these amazing people. Eat BBQ ribs and cakes. Drink one beer and feel like I'm 4 deep. Thanking and hugging. Rinse & repeat. Local brewery with a bunch of friends. Can't believe all these people would come for us. Drink half a beer. So exhausted. Hotel to sleep. Older brother feeds me pizza rolls as last supper. Final night as Unmarried Bachelor Fiance Paul. Goodbye Unmarried Bachelor Paul. Hello Husband Paul. Hello Joyful Paul. Thank you God for this amazing woman. My wife. These are the end of these posts. Thank you for tolerating. NO WAY IN HELL I'M POSTING NIGHT OF WEDDING. XOXO.

Post Wedding Night:

It was pretty short.

BUT NOT AS QUICK AS YOU'D EXPECT.

I was way too excited and couldn't stop mentally high-fiving myself. "You're doing it, buddy, you're having sex. Right. Now. If only you could see yourself. Can't believe this is happening."

We both cried. It was beautiful.

The end.